The SECRET ENERGY of YOUR BODY

An Intuitive Guide to Healing, Health and Wellness.

(SECOND EDITION)

By Dr Irina Webster

Copyright © 2021 (Irina Webster)
All rights reserved worldwide.

No part of the book may be copied or changed in any format, sold, or used in a way other than what is outlined in this book, under any circumstances, without the prior written permission of the publisher.

Publisher: Inspiring Publishers,
P.O. Box 159, Calwell, ACT Australia 2905
Email: publishaspg@gmail.com
http://www.inspiringpublishers.com

 A catalogue record for this book is available from the National Library of Australia

National Library of Australia The Prepublication Data Service

Author: Irina Webster

Title: The Secret Energy of Your Body:
    An intuitive guide to healing, health and wellness

Edition: 2nd

ISBN: 978-1-922618-04-7 (print)
978-1-922618-05-4 (ebook)
978-1-922618-06-1 (hardcover)

Subjects: Intuition.
    Healing.
    Health.
    Spiritual healing.
    Mind and body.
    Therapeutic use.
    Energy medicine.

Dewey Number: 615.852

TABLE OF CONTENT

Introduction 7

My Intuitive Journey 9

CHAPTER 1: Essential Knowledge About Human Energy and Intuition 15

CHAPTER 2: Your Initiation to Sense Energy 22

CHAPTER 3: The 7 Steps to Intuitive Healing 25

CHAPTER 4: Healing the Mental, Emotional and Energetic Causes of Disease 40

CHAPTER 5: Intuitive Healing Guide to Physical Problems 49

CHAPTER 6: The Energetic /Emotional Meaning of Illnesses 156

CHAPTER 7: The Secret Energy of Your Emotions. How to Express, Release and Heal Your Emotions 209

CHAPTER 8: Emotions and Colours 215

CHAPTER 9: Understanding Negative Emotions 218

CHAPTER 10: How to Forgive 233

Afterword 236

About Author 237

Bibliography 239

DEDICATION

This book is dedicated to the wonderful lectures and professors in my two Alma Maters - Northern State Medical University (Russia) where I graduated as medical doctor and St Petersburg Pediatric Medical University where I did my post-graduation studies in Immunology and Allergy and where I was first introduced to the knowledge I describe in this book.

PREFACE

"The Secret Energy of Your Body" is not just a book; it is an important component of your prescription to wellness, health, happiness, joy and unconditional love. It is your guide to tuning into your body, looking inside and connecting to the Divine Energy that we all consist of. This book is dedicated to combined science and spirituality. Since 1994 I have researched and collected scientific data on how emotions affect organs and create symptoms.

This book is based on my extensive research and years of experience in the medical field. I have spent years developing and implementing this original programme to help thousands of people overcome their medical issues where traditional medicine failed to help, and heal not only their bodies but their spiritual selves.

INTRODUCTION

"Energy is the root of body and mind. When energy flows through the body properly, you are in a state of health.

When there is an energetic disturbance in the body, a disease state is created.

Illnesses manifest in the body's energy field before they manifest in the physical body, and healing occurs in the energy field before it becomes apparent in the physical body.

The root cause of the energetic disturbances that cause many physical ailments is frequently negative thoughts, limiting beliefs and destructive emotions stored in the body."

I live by the motto that healing is always possible. Even if your wounds are deep or the illness is severe: believe in healing. This allows you to release the energy of long-held fears and negative thoughts even though one's body may be dying physically.

You can heal yourself simply by reversing your mental and emotional patterns, changing lifestyle, altering behaviours and changing attitudes. It is possible because your emotions and thoughts are linked to your body via the immune, endocrine, and nervous systems which control the state of your health.

How does it work?

All your thoughts and emotions are energy and they activate a physical response in the body. A fear for example activates every system in the body; your stomach tightens, your heart rate increases, your skin sweats and your muscles contract.

A loving thought on the contrary, can relax your whole body.

Repeated thoughts stay in your cells and eventually become your cellular memory. When there is too much negative energy in the same cells, this part of the body gets sick.

Therefore your body becomes a direct reflection of your thoughts, emotions and experiences. Your body tells everything about you. Your pains, aches and symptoms are simply messages to show you that something isn't working in your body. Their purpose is to get your attention, to make you tune into your body and ask, "What's going on? Is there a message you're trying to send? "

Then, listen to the answer....

This book will show you how to listen to your body and heal it by sensing and manipulating the body's energy. It will also teach you how to talk to your body by understanding energy signals. This book is not just about how to survive through problems, it is also about how to thrive and blossom in any circumstances you find yourself in.

I will show you many healing techniques that are simple but very powerful. Implementing them can bring you great health, lasting freedom, strong faith and a state of flourishing in this difficult world.

MY INTUITIVE JOURNEY

My name is Irina. It's a Russian variant of Irene which means 'peace'. I love my name because for me 'being intuitive' means being at peace with myself, and seeing things from a peaceful point of view.

I am a healer, a medical doctor and an intuitive. For over 20 years I have been helping people heal. For the last 5 years I've taught intuitive healing and intuitive development. I came to do this after having several self-healing experiences when I used my own intuition to heal myself, and I even saved myself from having dangerous surgery and invasive medical treatments. I'll tell you all about this later in the book.

Before I started teaching intuitive healing I worked as a medical doctor for 14 years, practicing Paediatrics for about 10 years in Russia (my birth country) and then working in General Practice area for about 4 years in Australia (my second homeland).

I have been intuitive for as long as I can remember. Even as a child, I was able to sense energy around people, although at that time I couldn't explain what it was. I could just feel if people were kind or not, sick or healthy. I also felt how other people affected my body; I could experience physical pain in my body when in contact with certain people or absolute serenity and joy when with others.

I had visions nobody could see. I sensed energy around people and described it in colours.

"Aunt Galina always looked green like a spring leaf on a birch tree." – This is what I noticed about my aunt who was a Pulmonologist (lung specialist) and also a great healer.

"Grandpa is so grey and brown." This is what I noticed about my grandpa who was dying from old wounds he got during the war.

Becoming a doctor was my intuitive decision. I really wanted to learn what goes on inside my body and why I have these strange experiences regarding others and myself.

Studying at university and working as a doctor gave me a clear understanding about the anatomy, physiology and biochemistry of the human body and what happens to the body when people get sick.

Unfortunately, it didn't give me the answers I needed about intuition, energy, or healing. For a long time I had to hide the fact that I am an intuitive who can feel people's energy. You see, conventional medicine doesn't recognise the fact that human energy exists and plays a crucial role in human health. Due to these reasons I found myself having an internal conflict between what I knew and what I felt.

But, fortunately, the Universe granted me several challenges that reunited me with my spirit and with the 'subtle energy' we all are made of.

How it all began

Eating Disorder and my first encounter with the 'subtle body energy'

When I was a teenager, I was overweight and was bullied at school because of my weight. I tried many methods to lose weight and was constantly on a diet, which, of course, was no fun. As a result of this bullying over my weight issues, I developed a severe eating disorder by the age of 14. Over the next 10 painful years, I was alternating between anorexia and bulimia. During this time, I lost a lot of weight, was skeletal and my period even stopped for a year because of malnourishment. Sadly, conventional treatments did nothing for me. In short, my health was in serious trouble.

I was always a very sensitive person and I spent a lot of time alone due to how my eating disorder made me feel. One day in my early 20's when I was studying to become a doctor at Uni, I found myself in a lot of pain. My stomach and my back were in agony. I didn't want to take normal painkillers such as Nurofen or Aspirin that upset my stomach and Paracetamol wasn't effective.

Without the influence of pain medications and with my pain rising, I sat on my bed holding a pillow. I started to swing back and forth trying to get into the rhythm of my pain. I don't know how long I was swinging back and forth hugging the pillow before I realised that I was actually in a different state of consciousness.

Soon, instead of the pain, I started to feel tingling in different parts of my body. This new sensation was pleasant and felt similar to a mild electric current. At this point, I also noticed that I was able to transfer the energy current in my body to different areas of my body simply by redirecting my attention from one part to another.

What astonished me was that I could also see my organs from inside. The new mental and physical state I was in had actually opened up a new way of seeing the human body. When I moved my attention to my stomach, where I had what could accurately be called extraordinary pain, I saw a red inflamed lining with little ulcers around it. This was likely due to the continual vomiting.

Looking closer and more intently, I noticed that when my attention was on my stomach it was tingling with energy. The sensation was actually calming and pleasant. I played with this energy like a child.

I don't know how long I was sitting in this state, but I eventually fell asleep. When I awoke in the morning, the pain was gone, simply gone, as if it had never existed in the first place. I felt refreshed and I felt completely different; I was transformed!

My urges to binge and purge were completely gone. When I thought about bingeing-purging, my body quickly responded, "Oh, no – not me. I am not doing this ever again." My entire being, mind, body and spirit supported me in healing the eating disorder. Never again did I have the urge to binge-purge and my stomach was free of the problematic hunger pains.

Later on I realised that this was my first experience of feeling my subtle body energy which is a vital component of intuitive healing.

Uterine Fibroids – saving myself from having surgery.

The second time I healed myself was from an equally serious disorder. I was scheduled to have surgery for a uterine fibroid, but my body had other plans. I was 36 years old. At the time, I was highly stressed as I was working as a doctor in a hospital. Long hours and night shifts were commonplace. After a time, my body said 'enough' and simply rebelled, I developed very severe uterine bleeding, and frighteningly enough, was bleeding continuously for many weeks. When I went to see a doctor, I was diagnosed with a uterine fibroid, which is a benign growth inside the lining of the uterus. It is not cancerous, but trust me it was extremely painful. My gynaecologist told me that to control the bleeding I would need an operation, he felt that without surgery I would bleed to death. At that moment something quite powerful happened, as he spoke, a small quiet voice inside me said, "Don't go, don't go." It wasn't a loud voice; it wasn't a voice that made me scared or created fear. It was a very calm and subtle voice from inside my body.

I didn't argue with my gynaecologist. I took the operation referral and the drug script which he gave me. I went home and I had only one thought in my mind – 'I need to experience the healing state again.'

So I did. I sat down to heal myself. I went to a room where there was total peace and quiet and I was alone. I began to meditate. Once again, I felt tingling sensations in my body just as had happened during my first intuitive healing experience. Next, I moved my attention to my uterus. During my meditation, I could see a small tumor inside the lining of my uterus, I knew that it was this tumor that was causing the bleeding. Then I saw a green light inside my uterus, and this green light (like a laser) was cleaning my uterus from the inside. Finally, I sent lots of love to my uterus and to all my body. The experience was very calming, loving and pleasant.

The next day, my bleeding was much better. It was reduced by half or even more. I continued to perform intuitive healing two to three times a day. On the third day, the bleeding was gone completely; I have never had this problem again.

Again, sensing my subtle body energy saved my health.

Eczema – it was said to be a chronic condition but it never came back again.

When I was about 38, I suddenly developed very bad dermatitis, or eczema which affected my hands. I had an itchy rash on my hands which progressed to multiple blisters which in turn burst. The end result made my hands look like pieces of raw-meat. Doctors prescribed a steroid cream as well as antihistamines, I was told that this condition would probably come back again and again.

Being a healer in my soul, I always like to try healing first, so I did. I put myself into a healing state of consciousness and asked the Divine Healing Power to intervene and help me to heal my hands. I focused my attention on my hands and felt how the healing energy was repairing my skin with love and gentleness. At the end of the meditation, I sent lots of love to my hands and felt extremely grateful for the divine healing.

The next day, I had major improvement with the eczema. On the fifth day of healing, both my hands were absolutely clean. The condition has never returned.

I truly believe that in order to heal, one must be in touch with one's own energy. The same goes for all the other things in life such as relationships, wealth and career.

My connection to Psychoneuroimmunology.

In my early years of being a doctor, I had a great interest in immunology and even did my post-graduation studies in this field acquiring a qualification of children Immunologist –Allergist from the Medical University of Saint-Petersburg (Russia). During this time from the early 90th, I had my first connection to a new science called Psychoneuroimmunology (Psycho means psyche, neuro is for nervous system and immunology is for immune system). This science shows the connection of the psyche (emotions) and immune response from the physical body.

From this time, in the early 90th, I started collecting the scientific data of how Emotions – Organs – Symptoms are connected. I use this data in this book.

Chapter 1
Essential Knowledge about Human Energy and Intuition

If you break down your body to the smallest particles, eventually you get just energy. Our thoughts and emotions are also energy.

This explains why emotions are catchy. You can catch emotions from other people without even being aware of it. For example, if your friend is upset, your mood dives, if your partner is happy, you feel even happier. You don't need to even think about it – it happens automatically.

Sometimes, we can read each other's thoughts. Have you ever thought about a person and a few minutes later they call or you meet them at the shop? These are simple examples of how we sense energy in everyday life.

How do we sense energy?

Your regular thoughts and feelings create energy that surrounds you. It is your aura. Some people can sense auras. With a bit of training most people can do this. All humans are born with intuition which includes the ability to sense energy, but because we are programmed to use logic instead of intuition most people lose this ability.

Let's try a simple experiment which might enable you to sense your own aura (energy).

Rub your hands together for 30 seconds. Then bring them gently apart, like you're holding a ball. Then try to slowly bring them together. When you're bringing your hands together you start to feel resistance between your hands, it may feel like you are holding 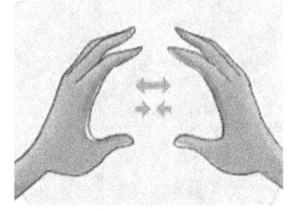 a ball, you may also feel a 'push-pull' sensation between your hands.

What you sense is your own energy activated by rubbing your hands.

Another way to feel this energy is by breathing into your hands

Sit down and relax; put your hands on your lap palm side up. Inhale deeply and exhale pushing the air through the palms of your hands, repeat it 5-7 times. Focus on your hands during breathing, notice the sensations. If you have any tingling, crawling sensations or warmth- this is your subtle body energy.

The more you feel it, the more sensitive you become to the energy around you. With practice you'll be able to sense the subtle energy in any part of your body, this is essential for healing.

How does your mind perceive energy?

Our mind has two parts – the intuitive and the logic mind. We sense energy with the intuitive mind. Let me explain...

We use the logic mind to think, analyse, plan, compare, judge etc. The information we receive from this part of the mind is structured, rational and based on our previous knowledge.

The intuitive mind gives access to information which is not logical, rational or organised in any particular way. This information is spontaneous, unlimited, not rational and unplanned. Intuitive information can only be accessed when we are able to get our logical mind out of the way.

The intuitive mind is the biggest part, and takes about 90% of our whole mind capacity.

The logic mind takes up only about 10% of our entire mind's capacity. That's why scientists often say that during our life we only use

10% of our mind's capacity and the rest is unused.

From childhood we are programmed to use logic and ignore intuition. We are taught to use just the smallest part of our mind and disregard the biggest.

The intuitive mind is also much more complex then the logic mind, it consists of two parts: Subconscious and unconscious.

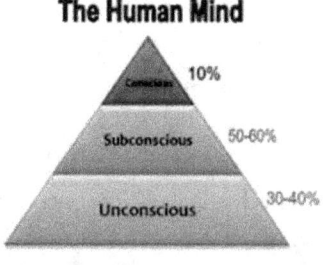

The subconscious mind refers to our feelings, emotions and senses. The unconscious mind refers to the unconscious processes in our body such as digestion, respiration, perspiration, body temperature, waterworks, pulse, heartbeat, tissue growth, regeneration, blood pressure, metabolism, hormone production, etc.

Our behaviours and deep beliefs are located in the subconscious mind. That's why when we try to work on a health or a relationship problem just from the logical mind point of view, we don't get anywhere. We must address these problems from the subconscious mind –from our emotions and feeling's point of view to create lasting positive changes in our health and wellbeing.

How do people sense intuitive information?

Everybody senses intuition in a different way. You should start paying attention to the unique ways you feel energy and receive intuitive information.

Intuitions often come suddenly and unexpectedly, it's instant and spontaneous. It can come as a flash of ideas, energy changes in the body, pictures, colours, inner knowing, a memory or a dream.

People often dismiss intuitive information because it's so quick and subtle, plus our brain chatter, (which comes from the logic mind), is loud and intrusive, most of the time. This is the reason why most people miss their intuitive messages. Unless you learn to slow down your logic mind, you will struggle with intuition.

Regular meditation is the simplest and most reliable way to slow down the thinking mind.

How to differentiate intuitive messages from fear and brain chatter

Many people have difficulty differentiating the voices of intuition from the voices of fear and brain chatter.

Brain chatter and the voices of fear are loud, continuous and emotional voices. They are critical and judgmental. They often refer to your past negative experiences, saying things like, "when was the last time I did this ......" or "when my friend did that ....".

The table below shows the differences between irrational fear/brain chatter and reliable intuitive information.

Signs of Fear and Brain Chatter	Signs of Intuition
It brings emotionally charged information. It is negatively or positively charged. It is judgemental/critical or artificially happy/excited.	It brings information in a neutral, unemotional way, like seen in a movie.
It reflects past experiences- negative or positive and goes over and over again about the same things.	It brings detached sensations, not necessary based on previous experiences, like you're in a theatre. It is spontaneous and comes in a flash.
It diminishes centredness and perspective.	It brings centredness and the sense of knowing.
The voice is loud.	The voice is subtle, quiet and calm.
It comes from your head (brain).	It comes from your body, usually from the centre of the body – gut or chest, but it can come from any part of the body.

Human energetic anatomy

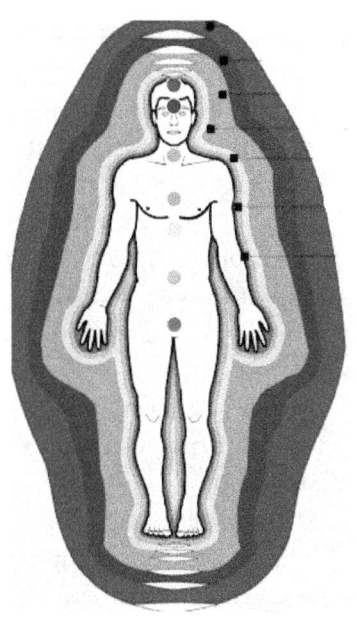

As well as having physical anatomy, we also have energetic anatomy. The energetic anatomy is very precise and it contains the energy of all experiences we have had in life. It has three main elements: Chakras, meridians and aura.

Chakras are the energy centres in our body. There are seven major chakras and they are located in the middle of the body.

Meridians are the channels where energy flows from one body part to another.

Aura is the energy field around the body. Aura is a reflection of the chakras energy. The quality of the aura depends on your health, past experiences, environment, lifestyle and how you enjoy your life. The aura changes depending on the kind of thoughts and feelings you have.

Healthy and happy people have vibrant and bright auras.

Sick and unhappy people have heavy, dark or weak auras.

If you have an illness in a particular part of the body, your aura gets depleted or contaminated in a specific way. You will notice energy depletion or contamination around a sick body part.

What is intuitive ability?

When I talk about intuitive ability, people imagine widely differing ideas about what "intuitive" means. Some people think that it includes extraordinary talent to know all things at all times. Others think it's like having X-ray vision. Some people think it gives you the ability to know the future or the past. Some people believe it means seeing ghosts or talking to dead people. Some people think it's a great power.

Intuitive ability can mean different things to different people. So let me begin by explaining what I mean when I say "intuitive ability".

For me, being intuitive means the ability to sense energy which is around us and inside us. It is the ability to look at someone and see what energy they carry inside and who they really are and recognise their soul. It is the understanding that our true essence is energy, and that our physical body is our instrument to express this energy, just like a piano is an instrument to express music. The piano is a tool for music expression, but without a skilled pianist, the piano may sit silent.

The same is true for people. We are here on Earth to realise and express our divine energy. Our body and mind are our instruments of expression.

The ability to sense energy is inborn but many people have lost it because we are programmed to use logic instead of intuition. But with a bit of training this ability will come back to you. I guarantee!!!

Look at your life experiences and you'll find that you have already felt energy many times, (but maybe didn't pay enough attention to value it).

1. When you are around some people do you feel drained?
2. Have you ever felt that someone was staring at you?
3. Have you ever felt instant liking or disliking for someone?
4. Have you ever been able to sense how someone is feeling, in spite of how this person was acting?
5. Have you ever felt a 'gut instinct' regarding what's ailing a person?
6. Have you ever been able to sense another person's presence before you actually heard or saw this person?
7. Do certain sounds, colours and fragrances make you feel more comfortable or uncomfortable?
8. Do you find that some people excite or energise you more than others?
9. Have you ever walked into a room and tightened up, fidgeted or felt angry? Do some rooms make you want to stay? Leave?

10. Have you ever ignored or shoved aside a first impression of someone, only to find that it bears itself out eventually?
11. Are some rooms more comfortable and enjoyable to be in than others? Do you notice how your brother's/sister's room feels different from yours? How about your parents' or children's?

If you answered "Yes" to any of these questions – you have experienced the energy of other people. With more training and practice you will begin to feel more subtleties in other people's energy including the subtleties in your own energy. With training you will become more and more intuitive.

Therefore, listening to your body messages helps us to save (and restore) our health, our relationships, our happiness and even save lives.

Chapter 2
Your Initiation to Sense Energy

You must believe in your intuition and in your own power. This is your first step into the realm of intuition and energy.

What you believe about intuition determines your ability to heal and sense energy. Limiting beliefs block energy and stop you from healing. All doubt, negativity, resistance, judgement, rage and resentment can abort the healing entirely.

Look at your beliefs and attitudes and see if you have any blockages compromising your intuitive abilities. Where do the blocks come from? They usually come from the past. Some blocks we inherit from our family, the others we get from our friends, society and environment.

The most common intuitive blocks are:
1. Religious block. It is when people have been taught to believe in a powerful authoritarian God outside the human body. People start to believe that the body is fundamentally flawed and that you should seek authority outside yourself.
2. Intellectual block. These people may perceive intuitive messages but disqualify them as being coincidences, chance or luck and therefore not indications of true intuitive abilities. In this case you will continuously doubt your intuitive ability and always seek physical proof of intuition.

3. Low self-esteem block. This is when you already feel that you are intuitive but you don't find it very comfortable. You may sense energy and read situations more accurately than others but you feel self-conscious, like an ugly duckling. You may even feel burdened by being different.
4. Disorganisation block. These people are disorganised. They have no clear direction, no purpose in life. They live in a constant state of disarray, with unfinished business and for this reason they fail to perceive subtle energy. If you are not organised, you won't be able to become consistently intuitive.
5. Stress and anxiety block. If you are anxious, too much in a hurry and have a stressful life you will not be able to sense the energy around you.
6. Fear of intuition block. This is when you deny your feelings because you are afraid of the responsibilities associated with this ability. Intuitive healing assumes that you take all responsibility for your own health.

Believe that you're an Intuitive Person

You must believe in intuition. You don't need to prove it, you don't need to force it and you don't need to brag about it. You ARE an intuitive person.

To get the calm awareness about your intuition, use these autosuggestions:

I am open to intuitive guidance.
I will expect intuitive guidance.
I will trust intuitive guidance.
I will act on intuitive guidance.

Start an intuitive healing journal. You'll need a small portable notebook or notepad and carry this journal with you everywhere, and record all intuitive activity as it occurs. This includes all impressions, impulses, and what you might call coincidence. Do not censor, edit, or dismiss anything, everything counts. Whatever you feel, whatever comes to mind, just jot it down. Nothing is too petty, too silly, too stupid or too weird. Your journal is not supposed to sound smart although it might if you feel like doing that. Just listen to your inner dialog, connect to your body and to deeper places inside you. Your journal will eventually become like an intuitive therapist to you. In the end you will want to keep a record.

Make a sacred contract with your spirit about the process of healing and learning.

> **Contract with my spirit.**
>
> I, ..., understand that I am undertaking an intensive, guided encounter with my own intuition. I commit myself to the healing process. I , ..., commit to daily intuitive journal and fulfilment of each step in this book.
>
> I, ..., also commit myself to excellent self-care: Healthy diet, good sleep, and regular exercise for the duration of this intuitive healing process.

Chapter 3
The 7 Steps to Intuitive Healing

Over a 25-year period of working with patients (initially as a doctor, then as a healer), I have come to understand that intuitive healing process can be broken down into 7 consecutive steps. Initially, I followed these steps even without realising I was following them. I did it automatically. But when I started teaching and doing workshops about intuitive healing, I gave each step a name.

The 7 steps to intuitive healing:
Step 1: Tune into your body.
Step 2: Sense the subtle energy in your body.
Step 3: Visualise the structure of your body.
Step 4: Ask your intuition for help and guidance.
Step 5: Manipulate the energy with your hands.
Step 6: Use the energy of colours to counteract the problem.
Step 7: Listen to your dreams and visions.

Step 1: Tune into your body

There are two places you can be: In the mind or in the body. Culturally we are conditioned to be in the mind rather than in the body. When you are thinking, rationalising or planning you are in the mind.

When you are in the body you have a sensual experience: You sense it rather than think of it. It means experiencing the present moment with your senses without analysing or judging the experience.

During my workshops people ask me, "Why stay in the body, it's so miserable. My body aches and it's not healthy. What can I gain by being there?"

The answer is that every pain, ache and sensation has a meaning. Your body is a reflection of all your thoughts, emotions and feelings. Therefore, every pain contains the key to its cure. By listening to your aches and pains you'll help yourself heal.

My patient Sonya was addicted to smoking and tried to quit for a number of years, she also suffered from anxiety. She panicked especially when her father came to town, she got anxious, irritated and even had difficulty doing her work during these times and needed more cigarettes to 'calm' her nerves. She couldn't understand why she felt this way because generally, her relationship with her father was good. She told me that her father left the family when she was 11 years old and she saw him every second weekend after that.

I explained that her body was giving off signals and she must listen to them in order to understand why. She said that she was afraid to listen to her body because it felt miserable, but finally she agreed. During one of the sessions she had a memory emerge. She remembered that when her father left the family she felt deep regret and felt like a part of her body separated from her. Although she saw her father every second weekend she felt extremely jealous especially when her father announced his engagement to another woman. As a teenager she started smoking in order to feel closer to her father, when they smoked together they had open conversations.

She stopped smoking on the same day. She realised that she doesn't need to smoke in order to be close to her father. Her anxiety gradually ceased.

By tuning into her body she found a cure by understanding the primary reason for her smoking and anxiety.

I noticed this happens often: When people bring meaning to their pains they become guided to heal. Pain is necessary for us to protect ourselves, its purpose is to focus our attention onto the problem. When we understand the pain, we are able to heal it.

The process of tuning into the body:
1. Sit down and breathe.
2. Focus your attention on the painful spot or on a particular organ.
3. Breathe through the spot and keep your attention inside the body.

Step 2: Sense the subtle energy of your body

Sensing your body's energy is essential for healing. Your body's energy can reveal a lot of hidden information such as cellular memories. Every cell responds to your thoughts, feelings and behaviours, you can release the negative cellular memories when you sense their energy.

Sensing subtle energy can help you stay healthy. Diseases never appear just out of blue, subtle changes precede most physical symptoms. If you catch imbalances in your body before you have pain or a full-blown disease you can stop the problem before it begins.

Look at Maria's story...

Maria suffered gallstone attacks a few times a year. She often ended up in hospital on morphine. Her doctor recommended surgery but she didn't want that. I taught Maria how to sense and observe her subtle body energy. As a result of this observation she noticed something quite interesting. She noticed that for a day or two before an attack her abdominal area would feel bloated and warm, these special sensations only came just before an attack. She used this new found knowledge and the next time she felt the same feelings she took the medicine. From that day her gallstone attacks became less and less severe and finally she managed to stop them for good. This skilful observation of her own energy changes in her body broke the pain cycle before the actual symptoms occurred.

Sensing such fine energies takes time and attention. It means noticing every subtle vibration in the body. These vibrations can take different forms like pictures, visions or emotions. People have shared with me impressive descriptions: The shop manager who felt as if he was stabbed in the back; the young woman with a black cloud over her heart; the housewife with a hole in her chest. You may have had similar powerful images.

The examples are many. You may experience strange feelings that parts of your body are congested, blocked or shut down with no physical evidence to support it, or the feelings that a segment of your body is amputated, empty or broken. That grey sadness in your chest, or red anger in your liver.

Subtle body energy is never wrong. It tells you about everything. It tells if your relationships are right or wrong, it informs you about your work and the environment you're in.

For example, have you ever met someone at work or at party and liked him/her immediately? It was not what they did, but you just liked to be surrounded with their energy. Or what about a person who seemed always nice but you constantly felt drained being with him? You just responded to his energy. Other people's energy can influence your wellness in a very real way. You must be aware of this and try to surround yourself with others who feel good to be with.

How to recognise if your encounters with others are positive or negative?

Subtle energy changes when your encounters are positive:
- You feel comfortable with the person. You sense the energy of brightness and openness.
- You have pleasant deja-vu moments - a sense that you have known the person before.
- You feel completely relaxed and you breathe easily. Your belly, chest and shoulders and throat are relaxed.
- You find yourself leaning forward, like you want to be closer to this person.
- Your heart feels open; you feel safe, secure, energised and alive.
- You like the person's touch. Their energy feels pleasant to you.

Subtle energy changes when your encounters are negative:
- You feel sick in your stomach like you have been punched.
- You can experience negative deja-vu moments – they are unpleasant or even scary.
- Your body feels tight. Your shoulders and chest are tense, your throat constricts.
- You may notice unexplainable aches, pains or weakness anywhere in your body, especially in your limbs.
- You experience creeping sensations on your neck, back and scalp.
- You are sensing sudden feelings of fear, depression, anxiety or darkness.
- The person's touch feels very unpleasant to the point that you instinctively withdraw if touched by this person.

Being aware of these signs can help you protect your energy when interacting with others.

The process of sensing subtle body energy:
1. Sit down and breathe.
2. Focus your attention on the painful spot or on a particular organ.
3. Breathe through this spot and keep your attention inside the body.
4. Notice any tingling, crawling sensations, or energy changes in the spot you are focusing on. This tingling is your body's subtle energy.

Step 3: Visualise the structure of your body

For healing it is important to visualise the organs you are working with. I recommend you to get a basic human anatomy book, and refer to it when you are doing healing. Alternatively you can use Google search. Just type a name of the organ and 'anatomy'. You will come up with many pictures that show what this organ looks like from the inside.

You don't need to be an anatomy expert but it's important to know that your heart has four chambers, and that your liver has two lobes in case you are trying to heal these organs.

Visualising the structure of your body helps you to be more precise with your actions, it helps to know where to remove the negative energy from or where to put the positive energy in.

There is an ancient ritual among Iglulic Eskimos in which a shaman uses his power to, 'divest his body of his flesh and blood' so that nothing but his bones remains. Then he recites all the parts of his anatomy and speaks aloud each bone by name. He gains power and self-knowledge by honouring every structure of which he is composed.

This will work for you too. Becoming conscious of your structure will help complete your self-image, bring awareness to your body and help heal the disease.

Step 4: Ask your intuition for help and guidance

We all possess an intuitive voice that contains answers about our healing, wellness and what is right for us. Some people call it angels, inner voice or a higher power. Whenever I am confused about an issue in my life and need direction, I ask for intuitive guidance. Sometimes I get a direct answer, sometimes a symbol, a picture, a vision or an idea. Often I experience immediate "Aha!" moments or instant reassurance from an invisible source.

You only need to ask a question or ask for guidance and you will get an answer in one form or another.

How do you request guidance?

The best way to ask for intuitive guidance is to get in a state of silence. Silence bypasses the mind. Because our intellect is so loud, the intuitive voice often gets drowned out.

What can you do to access your intuitive voice?

1. Learn to access the stillness within your body. You can access it through meditation, connecting with nature or through prayers.

2. Spend a few minutes each day devoted to listening to this voice. It may appear as a gut feeling, a hunch, an image, a sound, a memory, an instant knowing - as if a light bulb suddenly switched on.
3. Learn to ask specific questions. For example, "How can I deal with my difficult relationship?" or "What is the meaning of my shoulder pain?"
4 Learn to trust the signals your intuition sends.

Some tips when asking for intuitive guidance:
- Note your first impressions. As soon as you have asked your question notice your impressions without analysing. Write down the impressions, feelings, words or images you get even if they seem weird or don't make sense.
- Interpret your impressions. Let the answer to your question be revealed as if you were reading a story. Don't force a meaning. You'll know when the answer is clear because it will feel right to you. A good follow up question would be, "does this feel true to me?"

Remember that intuitive information is always accurate; however, we can make mistakes in the interpretation. Don't get frustrated, be patient, have fun and always approve of yourself.

The process of asking for intuitive help during the healing process:
1. Sit down and take a few deep breaths.
2. Focus your attention inside the body - on the painful spot or on a particular organ.
3. Breathe through the organ or the painful spot.
4. Sense your subtle body energy: Any tingling, crawling sensations, or energy changes.
5. Ask: "Intuitive Healing Power, give me guidance on how to heal my body (or relationship, or a particular organ and etc)."

Step 5: Manipulate the energy with your hands

Energy sensitivity spreads over the body in a fairly predictable pattern. It starts with the hands, first the palms and then the backs of the hands; then the forearms, shoulders, forehead and then the rest of the body.

Because hands are the first to sense energy we can use our hands for energy healing. You can remove negative energy from the body with your hands, you can put positive energy in with your hands.

Healing with hands is based on the effect of bio-electromagnetism which has been proven by science. It can really work if applied correctly and with the right attitude. Your hands can heal you.

Energy healing with hands includes energy cleaning, and putting positive energy into the body.

How to do energy cleaning?

Energy cleaning can be done in two ways: Sweeping technique and Anticlockwise movement technique.

Sweeping technique – for energy cleaning

1. Rub your hands together for 30 seconds to energise them.
2. Put your hands, (or one hand), a few inches above the spot or organ you need to heal.
3. Sense the energy of this spot or organ.
4. Start sweeping movements with your hand (s) and remove the negative energy from this spot.
5. Throw the negative energy into a fire – a candle or an imaginary fire.

Anticlockwise movement technique – for energy purification

1. Rub your hands together for 30 seconds to energise them.
2. Put your hands, (or one hand), a few inches above the spot or organ you need to heal.
3. Sense the energy of this spot or organ.
4. Start anticlockwise movements with your hand over the spot as if you are scooping ice cream. (Note: do anticlockwise movements as if you have a clock on your body).

5. Throw the negative energy into a fire – a candle or an imaginary fire

When you perform energy cleaning, repeat the word 'Clear' to increase the intention of cleaning.

NOTE: Don't throw energetic toxins into a room, always burn it with a candle or in an imaginary fire. Unburned toxic energy can come back to you or to somebody else.

After cleaning the energy with these techniques, you can put positive energy into the body, (or a particular spot), to strengthen it.

How to put positive energy in the body?

Before you start putting energy into the body make sure you have done sufficient energy cleaning. You can put energy in only if the body is clean. This is a rule.

Putting energy in is done by doing a clockwise movement above an organ or body part. Just put your hand above an area and start a clockwise movement. If you need to add a specific colour, you need to visualise that your hands are transmitting this particular colour.

> *Remember:*
> Taking energy out of the body – anticlockwise movement.
> Putting energy into the body – clockwise movement.

Step 6: Use the energy of colours to counteract a problem

Colours are certain wavelengths of electro-magnetic energy seen through our eyes. Every colour has a different energy, vibrations and healing quality.

Every disease, emotion or illness also gives off certain energy and vibrations. For example, inflammation is associated with red while depression is associated with blue.

Different energies of colours interact with each other and produce specific results. Blue can calm a person while red can stimulate and energise. Green-blue can relive pain and orange can help to clean your throat and lungs.

Colour is one of the languages of the soul because it influences our mood and emotions and affects our well-being. Using and avoiding certain colours is a way of self-expression; it sheds light on our personality. Colours affect our perception: Light colours make a space look bigger while dark colours make it look smaller.

Colours have a symbolic meaning which is immediately recognised by our subconscious mind because they influence the flow and amount of energy in our body.

Colour healing can be used very effectively to treat many problems: Physical, emotional, and spiritual. It can be used through visualisation, wearing colourful clothes and jewellery, eating colourful foods, using house decoration and working with plants, using crystals and essential oils, colouring hair and using make-up, drinking water from a coloured glass and burning colourful candles.

When I do healing I use energies of colours and project them to the organs or body parts. I generate a certain colour by rubbing my hands together, than placing them slightly apart and visualising a colour between my hands. Once I feel the vibration of a particular colour, I project this colour energy to the body part I am working with.

I also use colours to release emotions, boost vitality, increase confidence and bring peace. I have noticed that people who wear colourful clothes are happier than people who constantly wear black and grey.

I have also observed that wearing blue and white can help to experience more peace and relaxation. Green can help with mental and physical rejuvenation, especially green plants in your environment. Pink and orange can help to attract love. Red and gold is the best for boosting your energy and attracting wealth. Orange and gold can also stimulate your energy and bring feelings of abundance. Turquoise jewellery and blue clothes can help you become calm and confident. Lavender and indigo in your bedroom help to treat insomnia.

You can use the energy of colours to heal, thrive and prosper. It's very powerful, you just need to learn to sense colours and know the meaning of each colour.

Colour	Effect/meaning	Examples of use.
Black	Protection, strength and retreat. Too much black can depress and weaken the body.	- Combined with other colours it can assist in achieving your goals. - Promotes discipline, persistence and respect. - Helps to release the old and enter new experiences. - Can increase your strength. - Helps to resolve old patterns and let go.
Blue	Soothing, calming, inhibiting, cooling.	- Lowers blood pressure. - Slows a racing pulse. - Relieves headaches and migraines. - Relaxes eye strain. - Soothes earache and sore throat. - Stops bleeding. - Relieves fevers. - Calms anger and over excitement.
Brown	Protects, supports, provides structure. Too much brown can create dullness, fear of change and unwillingness to express your feelings.	- Helps to connect to the healing properties of nature. - Helps to revive your energy and creativity. - Helps create healthy boundaries.
Gold	Attracts abundance, expands mind and increases awareness. Promotes wisdom, self-confidence, inner strength, courage and joy.	- Assists in healing all illness. - Counteracts frustration, inadequacy and futility. - Helps to release any traumas. - Heals depression, scars, digestive problems, irritable bowel syndrome, menopausal problems. - Provides mental and emotional clarity.
Green	Cleansing, dissolving, disinfecting, healing, calming, decongesting.	- Revitalises nervous system, heart and liver. - Lowers blood pressure. - Stimulates growth of bones. - Disinfecting blood. - Cleans toxins.

Grey	Detachment, neutrality, solid, stable, calming.	- Helps to stay neutral when learning how to scan your body. - Assists with identification of blockages in a person's body or aura. - Helps with maintaining detachment when doing an intuitive reading.
Indigo	Promotes intuition, improves concentration, and facilitates energy sensing.	- Helps to release fears. - Promotes mental clarity. - Helps to heal eye problems. - Dissolves emotional confusion in adults. - Assists to release stress. - Gives a sense of clarity and direction in life. - Helps purify the blood and reduce excessive bleeding. - Improves sense of smell. - Acts as a painkiller.
Orange	Expelling, stimulating, detoxifying, triggering, initiating.	- Cleans throat, lungs, nose, ears and skin. - Heals digestive problems. - Awakens sexuality. - Relives constipation. - Stimulates happiness and confidence. - Relives allergies.
Pink	Promotes the energy of unconditional love.	- Heals grief and sadness. - Restores youthfulness. - Brings you in contact with your feelings. - Opens heart. - Brings self-acceptance and tranquility. - Promotes compassion, affection, warmth, friendliness, kindness, gratitude, generosity, strength and nourishment. - Helps to relieve menopausal problems.

Purple	Stimulating mental and intuitive qualities.	- Enhances senses: hearing, eye. - Sight and smell. - Releases negativity. - Promotes mental clarity. - Improves focus and attention. - Brings positivity and success. - Helps to connect with spirit. - Allows you to experience peace. - Evokes inspiration.
Red	Stimulating, dilating, expanding and growing.	- Stimulates a sluggish immune system. - Instantly boosts energy levels. - Stimulates reproduction and fertility. - Increases blood flow in organs and body parts. - Counteracts tiredness and lethargy. - Stimulates low blood pressure. - Promotes courage and strength.
Silver	Peace and persistence.	- Calms and brings serenity. - Expands awareness. - Strengthens the healing process. - Helps to flush toxicity from the blood. - Brings clarity.
Violet	Regenerating, balancing, harmonising, cleansing, energising.	- Regenerates nervous system. - Promotes spiritual development. - Balances all energies. - Helps to evoke a meditative state. - Harmonises the spirit. - Re-programs cells. - Activates intuition. - Opens creativity. - Helps to release karma.
White	Purifying, cleansing, balance, spiritual strengths.	- Assists in making choices. - Helps with honesty, purity, protection and reflection. - Supports in achieving dreams. - Gives mental clarity and balance. - Cleans skin problems.

Yellow	Purifying, cleansing, stimulating, detoxifying, triggering, hardening, initiating.	- Promotes tissue growth. - Eases arthritis. - Cleans skin. - Helps to repair wounds. - Helps with mental stimulation. - Helps to release toxins from any organs.

The process of using colours for energy healing:
1. Rub your hands together.
2. Place them slightly apart.
3. Visualise a colour and sense the energy of the colour with your hands.
4. Project this colour energy to the needed body part by placing your hand (s) over this body part, and then do a clockwise movement.

Step 7: Listen to your dreams and visions

Dreams provide answers about health, relationships, jobs or any new directions. The secret is to remember them. I suggest keeping a dream journal by your bed. Before you go to sleep, ask a specific question, for instance, "Should I stay in this relationship or should I move on?" or "How can I heal my anxiety?" or "How can I help my mother to get better?"

You can ask anything. But it's better to be more specific and state the problem clearly.

When I do it, I write a question down in my dream journal and meditate on it for 10-15 minutes. Then I go to sleep. The next morning, I write down the dream I had, then I interpret the dream.

The important thing is to write your dream immediately after waking. The longer you wait – the more you forget, dreams tend to disappear very quickly.

If you don't get any answers or the answer was inconclusive, try repeating the question every night for the next week until the answer comes.

The answer can be direct information of what to do, or it can be a symbol, an image or a word that helps you to solve the problem.

People can experience healing dreams. When this happens a person may go to sleep with an illness and wake up to find it completely healed. Or some people may receive specific information on how to heal an illness.

When we sleep our logic mind is shut and we have direct communication with our subconscious mind. That's why dreams have answers to the things the logic mind doesn't know about.

The main things you should remember about dreams:
1. Have a dream journal and ask questions before going to sleep.
2. Meditate and sense your 'subtle body energy' before sleeping. It will connect you to the Divine source.
3. Record your dream in a journal immediately after waking.
4. Pay attention to the images, symbols or feelings that grab you. Underline them in your journal.
5. Don't analyse and rationalise the meaning of a dream. You get more insight if you mediate on it or ask for an interpretation in your next dream. Notice any sensations, images or memories that arise during meditation or straight after. This will explain the meaning of your dream.

Chapter 4

Healing the Mental, Emotional and Energetic Causes of Disease

In this chapter you will find information about energetic/emotional meaning of an illness in different organs and body parts. You will learn how your body talks and how it guides you to heal.

Since 1994, when doing my postgrad studies in Immunology, I became interested in Psychoneuroimmunology (the science of Mind-Body-Spirit connection). Since this time, I have been collecting the emotional patterns that affect our organs and create diseases. In this chapter you will learn about these emotional patterns.

You will learn your body language which consists of feelings, senses, pains, aches and illnesses, you will discover the meaning to all your pains and symptoms.

You will realise that often intuitive guidance comes in the form of symptoms and illnesses. When your life becomes too stressful, joyless and hopeless, illnesses strike to change our tracks, make us rest, and bring our attention back into the body and other important aspects of life that give us joy and meaning.

Please use this information as a guide to help you find your own insights into your health.

How to use this guide?

This guide shows the energetic/emotional meaning to the problems in different organs and body parts. So, first read about each organ or body part you are having problems with. For example, if you have problems with your ankles, read the explanation about ankles.

Secondly, feel how this explanation relates to you. From my experience, the emotional meaning which is associated with each condition is correct in about 90% of cases.

Thirdly, you should proceed with the healing process. Most healing processes reflect the intuitive healing steps described in the previous chapters. Keep these steps in mind when you do any healing work on yourself or for others.

> Step 1: Tune into your body.
> Step 2: Sense the subtle energy in your body.
> Step 3: Visualise the structure of your body.
> Step 4: Ask your intuition for help and guidance.
> Step 5: Manipulate the energy with your hands.
> Step 6: Use the energy of colours to counteract the problem.
> Step 7: Listen to your dreams and visions.

Fourthly, you should do an emotional release for each negative emotion you experience. The process is described in the, 'Releasing Negative Emotions from Your Body' chapter.

In each healing process you are asked to relax your body and sense your subtle body energy. You will be asked to breathe through the painful organ and focus your attention on this area. You will be asked to stop your brain chatter that blocks healing.

What you will need to do?

In each healing process you will be asked to relax your body and sense your subtle body energy. Like I already explained earlier, subtle body energy is the electricity of your body cells and it can be sensed as tingling or crawling or sensations of warmth in the organ or body part. It is very healing.

You will be asked to breathe through the painful organ. To do that you need to focus on this organ/spot and consciously push the air through the body part while you breathe. Your own breath has the ability to balance energy flow in the area which you're focusing on.

You will be asked to stop your brain chatter or clear your mind. Brain chatter is a voice inside your head which is continuously chatting, criticising, judging etc. Buddhists call it 'monkey mind'. To heal yourself you must learn to stop your 'monkey mind' because it blocks healing.

Also you will be asked to repeat the word 'Clear,' during most healing processes. This word is used to set the intention to clear all density, pain, stress and constrains out from your body and mind. Your intention will assist you in taking greater control of your own energy. Setting intention begins with your focus and your attention to what you need to achieve.

Using Colours to Heal

During the process of healing you will be asked to visualise different colours. Different colours have different vibrations or energy, many colours promote healing and wellness if used appropriately.

For example, when you visualise red, you bring into yourself strong energy of passion, vitality and power, this is very useful if you currently feel depressed or have low energy. Red can help to heal wounds, induce tissue growth and cells regeneration. Red can heal many chronic illnesses which have been draining your energy away. On the other hand, red will not be a good option for someone who has anger problems because red can induce anger even more.

Blue colour can help to relieve acute pain, stop bleeding and reduce inflammation. But it is not good to use blue for depression as it will only exacerbate it.

When studying Psychoneuroimmunology (the science of Mind-Body-Spirit) in the 90th in Russia, I understood how the energy of colour affect our five senses. I noticed that some people not only see in colours but smell, taste and hear in colours. Later, during my career, I researched how to balance 5 senses to heal the body using the energy of colour. As a result of this research, I created "Chromotherapy Healing: The Secret Energy of Colour Cards".

I recommend you use my "Chromotherapy Healing: The Secret Energy of Colour Cards" that I have created to balance your 5 senses and heal.

You will need to release all charge, (negative and positive), and stay neutral when sensing energy. Grey is the best colour to feel and visualise when you need to initiate neutrality.

Many people ask me: "Why having a positive charge is not good?"

A charge means preconceived ideas. For example, a person might believe that being absolutely loyal to your family is a positive thing, however, if your relatives start demanding loyalty and push you to do things against your will, then their point of view can create a lot of grief for you. Therefore, a positive charge is anything that you consider as good, but it is not good for you, - you just had a positive charge about it.

So, you need to release all preconceived ideas and allow yourself to connect to your intuition which is the only true voice you have. I also want you to release strong expectations and charges. When you're driven by negative emotions such as anger, hate, fear, jealousy you become negatively charged. This stops healing. When you're impatient, want things badly and expect too much, you create a positive charge that also impedes healing. When you release all charges, positive and negative, you allow intuition to flow into your life.

You Must Take Responsibility for your Health and Healing

Intuitive healing assumes that you take all responsibility for your own healing. This healing begins when you realise that the causes of your problems are hidden within you, not outside of you. It is not just external factors such as nutrition, infections and living conditions that make you sick. There is something deeper inside a person that determines the development of a disease. These deeper factors are intimate emotions, ingrained beliefs and mind programming. These could have started as far back in time even when a person was conceived and even beyond that.

Responsibility does not mean blaming yourself for feeling sick, it is quite the opposite. It means beginning to listen to your body and releasing all the energy that contribute to this condition.

My hope is that reading this book will help you understand your body better. This book offers you many practical techniques to create harmony and healing. All the techniques are simple, easy and fast. Anybody can do them and get a great benefit. If you can breathe and relax, read and visualise, feel and sense, you can heal. I have worked with hundreds of people, using these simple techniques to satisfyingly heal many conditions: Physical and emotional, spiritual and mental.

Karen, a woman in her late forties, came to see me because of her anxiety, insomnia, recurrent cough and choking sensations in her throat. Occasionally she had pains and aches all over her body which her doctor could not explain. She was taking several prescribed medications to control her problems but they didn't provide any lasting help. She worked as a public servant for over 10 years. My first impression after seeing her was that Karen did not have the ability to protect herself at her job, her heart was in a state of alarm, she never learned to communicate properly.

When I shared my impressions with her she agreed, saying that she feels like a scapegoat at her work place. People often blamed her when something at work went wrong. When I asked her to tune into her own body and listen to it, she got a picture in her mind that hundreds of black leaches were attached to her skin and sucking her blood. I explained to her that this picture is a symbolic meaning of the situation she was in.

We started the healing process by working with her emotions of anger, sadness, frustration, depression and resentment. She also had to work on forgiveness a lot and had to forgive many people until she started to feel better. I showed Karen the process of changing her negative thoughts, releasing dark, heavy feelings she was carrying inside and installing the positive ones. The process of healing took a few months but finally Karen found the courage to quit her job and start working as a real estate agent; a job she likes and feels good about.

What was significant is Karen's willingness to use the healing process every day; she was dedicated to her health. Every time I spoke with her she reported improvement, she was excited to share with me all the little steps of improvement she experienced. Gradually, she became well: She stopped having insomnia and her cough and choking sensations were gone. She stopped taking medications and got committed to self-healing.

Prior to this, Karen had consulted several doctors, naturopaths, psychologists and counselors with little improvement. However, when she was able to take responsibility for her own health and understand what her body was trying to tell her, she changed her life and was able to heal. Instead of feeling like a victim she became empowered and reclaimed her wellbeing.

I have many examples of people being able to change their lives and improve their health when they were willing to look inside, listen to their body and respond to their body messages appropriately. Don't disregard these techniques because they seem too simple; I truly believe that simpler is better. If you understand the problem, then you can change it.

If you are still skeptical you need to take it slowly and let yourself try at least one step at a time. Just think of it like this: How far can you get being skeptical? But if you have faith, even as small as a mustard seed you can move a mountain.

I have asked you to take responsibility for your own health and make your health a priority. In the end only this will matter. If more people stick to the notion of looking after themselves properly and taking responsibility for their lives, we would eliminate many diseases, conditions and problems. Do you agree with me? If your answer is 'yes', then you are ready to begin. It would be exciting to hear about your improvements! Don't hesitate to let me know about your results and contact me via my website http://dririnawebster.com/ I am looking forward to helping you heal and transform your life into health and wellness. I have created many Intuitive Healing courses for different problems and individual needs. You can look at them on my website and choose what suitable for you.

Change Your Energy – Change Your Health

You can't heal your body using the same energy that created the illness in the first place. Your energy must change. Healing means 'being whole' and must include all aspects of life that keep you well and healthy. Here are the major lifestyle changes I recommend to my patients to change their energy to heal:

1. You must believe in yourself. Believe that you are a valuable being who deserves great health and wellbeing. Love yourself. Treat yourself as you would someone you love: a child or a lover. Everyday start your day looking at yourself in a mirror and saying, "I love you" and truly mean it.

    I recommend doing "I love you" exercise first thing in the morning. Use a bathroom mirror, look into your own eyes and say "I love you...(your name)" - 10 times. Keep repeating it until you start feeling Love inside you.

2. Listen to the messages your body sends to you. Recognise when you need to rest, sleep, exercise, play, have fun and work. What are your cycles? Disease comes in when people don't listen to their bodies and ignore their stress, tension, fear, being overwhelmed, anxiety and other negative feelings. It is best if you take a few minutes break every couple of hours and do stretching, meditation, deep breathing or a short exercise routine. It will make a lot of difference to your health and wellness.

3. Feel your emotions rather than keeping them buried. To feel emotions, you need to stop thinking too much; excessive thinking distracts you from feeling your emotions. Remember that your feelings hold the key to your health, they let you

know what is serving you and what is not, and if you are on the right track or not.

When you feel your emotions, you can remove the energy of these emotions from your body, so they don't get trapped and damage your organs and body parts. Follow the "How to Release your Buried Emotions" 13-steps process that I describe in the chapter 7 in this book.

4. Be aware of your breathing. Focus on your breathing as often as possible. Shallow breathing keeps your body in a stressful state, make sure that when you breathe your belly expands rather than your chest. Abdominal breathing promotes vitality, longevity, health and wellness.

    Focusing on your breath helps to stay present. When you are at peace, you are living in the present. How to achieve this desirable 'present state'? Here is a practical tip - after seven breaths, concentrating on the breath entering your nose, filling your belly, and then exhaling, you will be present. Try it now.... and see the results ...

5. Eat consciously. A balanced diet is important for good health, but make sure you don't go over the top with diets. Intuitive eating is the key. This is when you consult your own body to what exactly your body needs, how much, in what combination and when.

    I recommend you learn more about intuitive eating which is the healthiest way to eat and be well. I describe it in a chapter of my book "How to Heal Using Intuitive Healing. A journey to a whole you."

6. Exercise. Many people complain about feeling tired, depressed, stagnant and low energy. Daily exercise is the best way to stop these lousy feelings. Create your own exercise program and stick to it in order to become strong, healthy, lean and fit. Regular exercise will help you feel better, enjoy your body, have more energy, detoxify and heal. The more you move the more joy you get.

7. Use more colour in your life. Each colour has different vibrations which affect you in different ways. Use red to stimulate yourself. Yellow to feel happy, blue to cool down, pink and orange to feel love. Colour therapy is easy and accessible to everyone; people have been using it for centuries.

    I recommend using colors to balance your 5 senses: touch, smell, visual, hearing and taste. When we balance five senses, we achieve the state of synchronicity - the state of attraction. You can use my Chromotherapy Healing Cards to learn how to balance your five senses.

8. Feel grateful. I believe everybody has something to feel grateful about in their life. Feel grateful for what you have: Your family, your life, your house, your friends, your job or things you love. Look around and you'll find things to feel grateful about. The more you look with intention, the more you'll find. This intention to find the things you're grateful for will create more ease and happiness in your life.

    Energy of Gratitude and Love are the highest energetic vibrations that will improve your general energy instantly.

9. Surround yourself with happy people and laugh often. Humour is infectious. There is a saying, 'laughter is the best medicine'. Laughter triggers healthy physical changes in the body; it strengthens your immune system, boosts your energy, diminishes pain and protects you from the damaging effects of stress. Best of all, this priceless medicine is fun, free, and easy to use. Statistics show that a good hearty laugh relieves physical tension and stress, leaving your muscles relaxed for up to 45 minutes after. Laughter triggers the release of endorphins, the body's natural feel-good chemicals. Endorphins promote a sense of well-being and can even relieve pain.

    Find humour in your everyday challenges and experiences. Don't take your problems seriously. See a funny side in them. This alone can help you heal much faster.

Chapter 5

Intuitive Healing Guide to Physical Problems

A famous expression concerning mindfulness says: 'Energy flows where attention goes'.

Intuitive healing assumes that you need to bring your full attention to the place of the hurt, pain or disease. This kind of healing asks you to listen to your pain and get a message from it rather than ignore, suppress or reject it.

Since the early 90th when I did my postgraduation studies in Immunology in Russia, I started collecting the scientific data of how emotions affect our organs and cause problems. In this chapter you will find organs – emotions associations that come from many years of working with patients, studying scientific research and medical documents. You can find the bibliography of my research at the end of this book.

The healing techniques that I describe in this book are based on the effect of Bioelectromagnetism that has been proven by science. Bioelectromagnetism suggests that all organs and body parts vibrate with different energetic frequencies. By tuning into the energy of the organ, you can correct the flow of energy and heal the organ.

When healing organs or body parts, follow the 7 Steps to Intuitive Healing:

Step 1: Tune into your body.
Step 2: Sense the subtle energy in your body.
Step 3: Visualise the structure of your body.
Step 4: Ask your intuition for help and guidance.
Step 5: Manipulate the energy with your hands.
Step 6: Use the energy of colours to counteract the problem.
Step 7: Listen to your dreams and visions.

These 7 steps to intuitive healing are aligned with the principles of Bioelectromagnetism that are scientifically proven.

I use simple and short explanations of organs meaning depending on their function to make it understandable for people.

Abdomen:

Problems with abdomen suggest that you are struggling to digest your life, holding on to the past, judging and criticising yourself. You are feeling inferior and insecure, often anticipating trouble, thinking, "What the next day might bring?" Generally, you are focused on getting more and more of everything but it doesn't satisfy you and even makes you suffer from obsessive thoughts like, "What should I do with my life?" or "Where am I going with all these thoughts?" You want attention from others but are afraid of rejection. You often compare yourself with others, thinking that others are doing better then you.

Healing Technique:

Tune into your abdomen by taking a few deep slow breaths. While exhaling push the air through your abdomen. Relax and soften your abdomen as much as possible. Notice any sensations, tingling or energy changes inside. Visualise the organs inside: See their shape, size, colour and texture.

Rub your hands together for 30 seconds to energise them. Put your hands (or at least one hand) a few inches above your abdomen and sense the energy your abdomen is giving off. Start downward sweeping motions in your abdominal area. Visualise you are sweeping all the pain, discomfort, toxicity and density from the area. Throw the energy toxins in a fire, you can light a candle or just imagine a fire. Repeat the word 'Clear' a few times to strengthen the intention. Continue abdominal sweeping for 5-7 minutes or until you feel lighter.

Say, "Intuitive Healing Power, please release all fear, pain, insecurity, toxic thoughts, struggle and rejection from my abdomen. Please dissipate the negative energy that contributes to this condition. Thank you".

Feel your abdomen becoming lighter and lighter as the negativity is leaving.

To purify the energy of your abdomen, do anticlockwise motions with your hand(s) for 3-5 minutes or until you feel lighter. Throw the toxins into the fire.

Say: "Intuitive Healing Power, allow me to feel safe, secure, supported and protected. Please give me strength, ease and relaxation. Please allow the loving and empowering spirit to enter my body. Thank you... Thank you... Thank you..."

Visualise some pink energy of love and empowerment entering your body. Allow yourself to feel loved and empowered. Visualise your hands are transmitting a pink light of love, project this light onto your abdomen by doing clockwise motions with your hands in front of the abdominal area.

Say: "Intuitive Healing Power, please heal and regenerate my abdomen with love and empowerment. Please restore my health to maximum strength and vitality. Thank you."

When going to bed ask for a healing dream. Say: "I need a dream that gives me guidance to heal my abdomen and make me feel safe and empowered." Write it down on paper and put it under your pillow. In the morning record the dream and interpret it.

Emotional release: To complete the process of healing you must release the emotions of fear, frustration and rejection, you must work on forgiveness.

Colour therapy: Use green for dissolving and decongesting, use orange for rapid heavy duty cleansing, use pink to instil love.

Adrenal Glands:

The adrenal glands are linked to your sense of balance. If you have problems you may be feeling tired, exhausted and overwhelmed by your emotions. Your moods are changing like a yo-yo, one minute you're happy and enthusiastic, the next, sad and hopeless. Your anxiety and fear relate to not trusting the way you're going. You have probably lost your identity by being constantly in service to others and experience indecisiveness, defensiveness and a feeling of being stuck. Continuous life dramas make you feel depressed, empty and worthless.

Healing Technique:

Look up where the adrenal glands are located in the body. Visualise them. Tune into your adrenal glands by taking five deep breaths, when exhaling, push the air through your adrenal glands. Notice any sensations you feel inside.

Rub your hands together for 30 seconds until they tingle. Put your hand 6 inches from your adrenal glands and sense the energy they send. Start downward sweeping motions at this area, visualise you are sweeping all the toxicity and blockages from this area. Say, "Intuitive Healing Power, release all anxiety, stress, pain, toxic thoughts and struggles out of my adrenal glands." When you're sweeping, throw the energy toxins in a fire. You can light a candle or imagine a fire. Repeat 'Clear, clear, clear' to strengthen the intention. Continue sweeping for 5-6 min or until you feel lighter.

To purify the area continue with anticlockwise cleaning of the area: Put your hand(s) several inches from your adrenals and do anticlockwise motions. Feel the sense of cleanliness and purification in the area of your adrenals.

Say: "Intuitive Healing Power, allow me to feel safe, strong, supported and protected. Please instil strength, peace and stamina into my body. Allow me to love and approve of myself. Thank you... Thank you... Thank you..."

Visualise a bronze colour of energy and personal strength entering your body. Feel like you are becoming stronger and more powerful.

Say: "Intuitive Healing Power, please heal and regenerate my adrenal glands to their maximum health and wellness. Thank you."

When going to bed ask for a healing dream. Say: "I need a healing dream that helps me heal my adrenal glands and brings me peace and joy in life. Thank you." Write it down and put the paper under your pillow. Meditate for a few minutes and go to sleep. Record your dream in the morning.

Emotional release: To complete the process of healing you must work on releasing emotions of sadness, hopelessness and depression.

Colour therapy: You should work with colours that promote cleansing, use green and orange.

Ankles:

The ankles represent moving forward in live. Ankle disease connects to the feelings of carrying too many burdens and going in the wrong direction. You may be overwhelmed with responsibilities and feeling trapped. Having too many commitments all at once: Job, relationship and other projects, wanting to leave the situation but can't because of your sense of self-righteousness. You are denying the pleasures of life and feeling unable to follow your dreams.

Right Ankle:

Problems with masculine/physical energy. There is a male who dominates you and you're giving away your power to him. The other possibility is you are unconsciously following your father's negative views. Feeling overwhelmed with responsibilities and being unable to say 'no' to others, trying to make people happy and having no time for nurturing yourself.

Left Ankle:

Problems with feminine/spiritual energy. Having a female in your life who irritates you. Not listening to your intuition or your soul.

Too much focusing on the needs of others ignoring your own. Not nurturing yourself. Denying your body's needs.

Healing Technique:

Relax. Take 5 deep breaths. Tune into your ankle. When exhaling push the air through your ankle, sense the energy inside in a form of tingling or crawling sensations. If you have pain, tune into it and notice its temperature, intensity, colour etc.

Ask yourself: "What burdens do I carry on my ankles?" Notice any images, feelings or energy changes that come up. Don't analyse, just receive the answer.

Now rub your hands together for 30 seconds to energise them. Put your hand 6 inches from the ankle and sense its energy. Start sweeping motions and continue for 2-3 minutes. Feel that you are cleaning the area. Then, do anticlockwise motions to purify the energy in your ankle. Throw all the negative energy into a fire, a candle or an imaginary fire. Repeat the words "Clear, clear..." until you feel lighter.

Say: "Intuitive Healing Power, please release all pain, burdens and pressure from my ankles. Please remove all chains and limitations that stop my movements. Thank you." Visualise that a dark cloud is leaving your ankles, feel your ankles are becoming lighter and lighter.

Visualise your hands transmitting a green light. Transfer this green light to your ankles by doing clockwise movements with your hand above the joint. Feel your ankles vibrate with healing green energy.

Say: "Intuitive Healing Power, please instil strength and power into my ankles and into my whole body. Allow me to move in the right direction with confidence. I am strong, empowered and spirited. Thank you."

Before going to bed ask: "Can I have a dream that guides me to heal my ankles. Thank you." Meditate on this request for a few minutes and go to sleep.

Emotional release: To complete the process of healing you must work on releasing fear, frustration and being overwhelmed.

Colour therapy: You should work with colours that promote cleansing such as green. You will also benefit from working with pink that promotes self-love.

Anus:

The anus symbolises letting go of your waste. Problems with the anus mean that you are stuck in the past, can't let go old beliefs and regretting some of the decisions you once made. You carry guilt, anger and the feeling of loss and abandonment inside. You can't forgive yourself and others. You feel stuck, frustrated and betrayed. You think that everything you do is pointless or not enough, self- sabotage and fear plagues you.

Healing Technique:

Tune into your anus by taking a few deep breaths and focusing on the area. Sense the subtle energy around your anus. Feel for tingling or energy changes. If you have pain, describe it. Is it sharp or dull? Hot or cold? If the pain was an object, what would it be? Does it have a colour?

Ask yourself: "Where and in what way am I stuck in my life? Why can't I let go? Who can't I forgive? " Listen to the answers. Notice any sensations or images that might emerge. Don't judge, don't analyse, just receive the answer.

Say: "Intuitive Healing Power, release all the negativity, pain and blockages from my anus. Please release all negative feelings and wrong points of view that contribute to this problem. Thank you." Visualise that the dense energy of pain is leaving your anus.

Energise your hands by rubbing them together for 30 seconds. Start a downward sweeping motion with your hand above the anus area. Visualise that you are sweeping the negative energy away from this spot. Repeat the word 'Clear' a few times and throw the toxins into the fire, a candle or an imaginary fire. Continue sweeping for 3-5 minutes.

To purify the area do anticlockwise movements with your hand like you're scooping ice cream. Continue to visualise that you're cleaning and purifying your anus and removing all blockages from it.

Say: "Intuitive Healing Power, please instill clarity, confidence and self-esteem in my body. Allow me to feel safe, supported and protected. Let my spirit shine and let me move in the right direction. Thank you." Feel lightness in your whole body.

Visualise that your hands are transmitting an orange light. Transfer this light to your anus by doing clockwise movements with your hands above the area of your anus.

Say: "Intuitive Healing Power, please heal and rejuvenate my anus to its maximum health and vitality. Thank you."

Order a healing dream when you go to bed. Write this request on a piece of paper: "I want to experience a dream to help me heal my anus." Put this paper under the pillow. Meditate on it for a few minutes and go to sleep. Record your dream first thing in the morning.

Emotional release: To complete the process of healing you must work on releasing emotions of fear and guilt. Go through the forgiveness processes and forgive each person individually.

Colour therapy: You should work with colours that promote cleansing, use orange and green.

Arms:

Your arms represent embracing life. Arm disease means you have difficulty embracing life's experiences, having internal conflict and self-sabotage, problems accepting new things and refusing to change.

Right Arm:

Difficulty coping with the negative side of masculine energy. Who are these men who cause you problems? Do you feel like you are being controlled by them? Or do you try to control others? You may also suffer from perfectionisms and righteousness.

Left Arm:

Difficulty coping with the negative side of feminine energy. Some females are causing you problems. You feel overwhelmed with emotions and tend to carry other people's problems inside your body. Can't forgive and let go.

Healing Technique:

Relax by taking a few deep breaths. Tune into your arm. Breathe through the painful arm. Sense the subtle energy in your arm, notice any tingling or changes in energy flow. If you have pain, describe it in terms of its shape, temperature, colour and density. Ask your body: "Is there a message you are trying to send me?" Listen for the answer.

Then stand up and shake your arms as if you are trying shake off all the problems and difficulties from them.

Say: "Intuitive Healing Power, please remove all the pain, fear, anger, sadness and frustrations from my body and from my arms." Visualise that the stressful feeling is leaving your arms.

Now rub your hands together for 30 seconds to energise them. Put one hand 5-6 inches from the other arm and start downward sweeping motions. Visualise removing all the pain and negative energy from your arm. Throw the negativity into the fire. Repeat the word 'Clear' a few times until you feel clearer and lighter.

Then shake your arms again. Continue cleaning your arm's energy with anticlockwise movements. Visualise your arm is becoming lighter and stronger.

Say: "Intuitive Healing Power, please instil strength into my arms and into my body. Allow me to embrace my life with ease and grace. Thank you."

Visualise your hands transmitting an orange light. Transfer this orange light into your painful arm by doing clockwise movements with the opposite hand.

Say: "Intuitive Healing Power, please heal my arm and make it strong, healthy, vital and flexible. Thank you."

When you go to bed ask for a healing dream. Say: "Can I have a dream to help me heal my arm. Thank you." Write this request down and go to sleep.

Emotional release: To complete the process of healing you must work on releasing emotions of fear, control and frustration. You must go through the process of forgiveness.

Colour therapy: You should work with colours that promote cleansing, use orange and green. Also work with pink to instil love.

Arteries:

The arteries symbolise the flow of joy and love in your life. Problems mean that you have difficulties with expressing love, giving and receiving love. You block intimacy, feel disconnected from others and suppress your emotions. When dealing with life challenges you are forcing and pushing rather than letting things unfold. You focus more on the material world and ignore the world of spirit and intuition. You are unable to talk about your feelings; prone to self-sabotage and blame.

Healing Technique:

Sit and relax. Keep your hands on your lap palm side up. Take 5 deep breaths, and when you exhale push the air through your hands. Focus on your hands until you start sensing a tingling sensation in your hands. Tune into the centre of your body. Put your hands on your chest and say: "Intuitive Healing Power, please remove all the blockages from my arteries. Allow me to release negativity, change my point of view that contributes to this condition. Thank you."

Rub your hands together for a few seconds until they tingle. Put your hands a few inches from your chest and start a downward sweeping motion along your main artery: From the top of your chest down to your abdomen. Sweep up all the toxic energy and throw it into the fire. Use a candle or visualise a fire.

Repeat the word "Clear, clear, clear" to increase the intention of cleansing and purification.

Say: "Intuitive Healing Power please instil the feeling of love and joy into my system. Allow me to love myself and others unconditionally. Thank you."

Visualise your hands are transmitting pink light. Bring your hands closer to your chest and transfer this pink light to your main arteries. Bathe your arteries with the pink energy of love.

Say: "Intuitive Healing Power, please restore and rejuvenate my arteries to their maximum health and vitality. Thank you."

When you go to bed, say, "Can I have a loving dream that will heal my arteries and my life." Meditate on this request and go to sleep. In the morning record your dream. Stay loving and lovable.

Emotional release: To complete the process of healing you must work on releasing emotions of fear, hatred, control and criticism. Individually forgive each person who hurt you (including yourself).

Colour therapy: You should work with green and orange to clean your arteries. Work with pink to instil love.

Back:

The back symbolises your support and safety. Back problems connect to carrying unresolved emotions, conflicts and burdens inside your body. You have probably been feeling unsupported, unprotected, overwhelmed and insecure, experiencing difficulty in forgiving and letting go of past hurts.

Upper Back:

Too many responsibilities and feeling that you are responsible for everything and everybody else, doing too much and not having enough time for rest and pleasure. Not trusting people around you and thinking that people close to you don't care about you. Worrying and obsessing about making everything perfect.

Middle Back:

Stuck in the past and holding on to guilt. Not taking time to love and cherish yourself. Experiencing mood swings due to oversensitivity and worrying about what others might think of you. Not forgiving yourself and others.

Lower Back:

Worrying about finances, survival and paying your bills. Carrying too much anger and feeling like a victim, struggling with everyday issues. Trying to control the uncontrollable, focusing on the problems not on the solutions.

Healing Technique:

Tune into your back by taking 5 deep breaths. When you exhale push the air through your back. Arch your back backward, tense the back muscles for a few seconds and release the tension. Then arch it again and release. Repeat 5 times.

Now arch your back forward and keep the tension for a few seconds. Then relax. Repeat arching forward and relaxing your back 5 times.

Feel the difference between tension and relaxation. Sense the energy inside your back as tingling or a crawling sensation. Keep breathing through your back and focus on it. Empty your mind, if any thoughts come - gently push them away saying, "Not this thought, not this thought."

Become aware of which part of your back feels dense and blocked. Focus on this particular part and breathe into this spot for 5 minutes.

Say: "Intuitive Healing Power please release all burdens, blockages, struggle, suffering and victimhood from my back. Thank you." Visualise a dark cloud of negative energy leaving your back.

Rub your hands together for 30 seconds and visualise they are transmitting gold light. Put your hands on your back and transfer this gold light to your back. Bathe your back in this gold energy.

Say: "Intuitive Healing Power instil the feeling of confidence, joy, support and safety into my back. Thank you."

To heal your back it's important to feel safe and supported. Every morning you should repeat this affirmation three times: "I am safe, secure, supported and protected."

When going to bed, ask for a healing dream. Say: "I need a dream that can help me heal my back and make feel safe and secure. Thank you." Go to sleep and don't allow any thoughts to enter your head.

Emotional release: To complete the process of healing you must work on releasing emotions of worry, anger, fear, being overwhelmed and frustrated. Go through the forgiveness process and forgive each person who hurt you.

Colour therapy: You should work with green to clean negativity and gold to create abundance.

Bladder:

The bladder is an emotional storage bin for different emotions especially those related to your relationships. Bladder problems can imply you're feeling angry with the opposite sex or a partner, experiencing low self-confidence and having a wishy-washy mentality. You are probably annoyed, irritable, sad, guilty, feeling powerless and frustrated with your current situation and wanting to be somewhere else other than where you are. You have difficulty forgiving, thinking that everybody is after you and you must hide.

Healing Technique:

Tune into your bladder by taking a few deep breaths. Visualise it. Feel the sensations inside it. Breathe through the bladder.

Say: "Intuitive Healing Power, please remove the feelings of anxiety, stress and powerlessness from my bladder. Please release irritation and low self-confidence from my body. Thank you. " Visualise a dark cloud leaving your bladder.

Rub your hands together for 30 seconds to energise them. Put your hand(s) 5-7 inches from your bladder and feel the energy. Then, start a downward sweeping motion. Visualise you are sweeping away all the negative energy. Throw the negative energy in the fire, a candle or an imaginary fire. Repeat the word 'Clear' a few times to strengthen the intention. Continue sweeping for 5-7 min or until you feel lighter.

To purify your bladder do an anticlockwise motion with your hand. Feel the sense of lightness and purity in your bladder.

Say: "Intuitive Healing Power, please instil confidence, security, certainty and strength into my bladder. Let me feel powerful, spirited and strong. Thank you... Thank you... Thank you..."

Visualise your hands are transmitting yellow energy. Place them near your bladder and do clockwise movements to put energy in.

Say: "Intuitive Healing Power, please heal and rejuvenate my bladder to its maximum health and vitality. Thank you."

Before going to sleep ask for a healing dream. Say: "I need a dream that can guide me to heal my bladder and bring balance into my life and relationships." Write it on a piece of paper and put this paper under your pillow. In the morning record your dream.

Emotional release: To complete the process of healing you must work on releasing emotions of anger, being overwhelmed and frustration. Forgiveness is necessary to heal your bladder.

Colour therapy: You should work with green for cleaning, with yellow for stabilising, with gold for strengthening and empowerment.

Blood:

The blood represents the flow of life. Blood disease means you're experiencing lack of enjoyment and pleasure in life, holding onto feelings of guilt, shame, suspicion and resistance. Keeping your wounds open by not forgiving. You may be feeling suppressed by a partner or a family member or a close friend. Worrying about the future, giving up on your dreams and desires, feeling inferior and not worthy of good things, thinking that life has lost its meaning. Children with blood problems often feel confused about parental conflicts and take the energy of fights, guilt and shame into their body.

Healing Technique:

Sit comfortably. Place your hands on your lap palm side up. Tune into the centre of your body and breathe deeply and slowly for a few minutes. When exhaling push the air through your hands until you sense them tingling.

Ask yourself: "Who can't I forgive in my life? Who makes me feel inferior?" Listen to the answer... Notice any energy changes, images, feelings or thoughts that come. Don't judge, don't criticise, just acknowledge the answers.

To purify and strengthen your blood you need to sense the energy vibrations inside every structure of your body. Let's start from your hands.

Breathe into your hands and feel the energy as a tingling or crawling sensation. Mentally raise these sensations higher towards your elbows and then towards your shoulders. Feel both your arms are vibrating with energy.

Move your attention to your neck and feel the energy vibrations in your neck. Then sense the energy in your face and the back of your head... Feel your whole head is vibrating with energy.

Move your attention to your chest, and then go to your abdomen. Feel the energy vibrations inside your organs one by one.

Move your attention to your thighs, hips and upper legs. Then go to your knees, calves and shins. Move down to your ankles and feet... Sense the energy in your ankles and feet...

Some parts of your body may start to feel alive, more sensitive and energetic, this is good.

Now feel that your whole body vibrates with energy.

Say: "Intuitive Healing Power please remove all feelings of insecurity, shame, guilt and resistance from my blood. Allow me to release all worries and all points of view that contribute to this problem. Thank you." Visualise a dark cloud moving out from your body, you will feel lighter.

Say: "Intuitive Healing Power please instil joy, creativity, happiness and confidence into my blood. Help me to experience love, peace and freedom. Thank you. "

Visualise a red light is entering your body from the top of your head and it is spreading inside you through your blood system. Feel the energy and the power of this red colour inside you.

Say: "Intuitive Healing Power please heal my blood to its maximum health and vitality and allow me to feel happy and joyful. Thank you."

Before going to bed order a healing dream. Say: "I need to experience a dream that helps me heal my blood and brings joy into my life."

Write these words on a piece of paper and put it under your pillow. Go to sleep, and record your dream in the morning.

Emotional release: To complete the process of healing you must work on releasing guilt, shame, fear and low self-esteem. Forgive everyone who contributed to your problem.

Colour therapy: You should work with red to energise, with green and blue to clean, with gold to create abundance.

Bones:

The bones represent the structure of your body. If you have problems, you are probably feeling that your life is losing its structure. You are experiencing limitations, resentment, bitterness and blame towards yourself and others. You are not loving your body and not spending enough time cherishing it, being too hard on yourself and expecting too much of yourself. Bones weaken when you feel weak, lost or disempowered. Bones break when you reach a breaking point in your life and it is a sign that you must change your attitude towards yourself and others.

Healing Technique:

Sit comfortably. Tune into your body by focusing on your breath. If you have painful bones, breathe through them, visualise your bones.

Say: "Intuitive Healing Power please remove all limitation, resentment and bitterness from my bones. Please let go of the blame, judgment and high expectation from my body. Thank you." Visualise a dark cloud is moving out from your body. Notice how much lighter you feel.

Rub your hands together until they tingle. Bring your hand(s) closer to the painful bone and sense its energy. If you have a bone break, notice how different this energy feels compare to the healthy bone. If you have a weakened bone, notice the energy depletion at the spot of weakness. Scan the energy of each bone that needs your attention.

Start a downward sweeping movement with your hand along the problematic bone. Visualise you are sweeping away all negativity, toxins and blockages from it. Repeat the word 'Clear' a few times to strengthen the intention of the cleaning.

Purify the bone by doing anticlockwise movements with your hand over the bone for 3 minutes.

Visualise your hands are transmitting a green light. Green stimulates bone growth so it is beneficial for healing. Bring your hands closer to the bone and transfer the green light to it. Do a clockwise movement with your hand to put the green energy into the bone.

Say: "Intuitive Healing Power please instil safety, security and love into my bone. Assist me to become confident, strong and powerful. Thank you."

Visualise your hands are transmitting a yellow light which has cementing qualities. Repeat the same process with the yellow light as you did with green light.

Say: "Intuitive Healing Power please heal my bones to their maximum strength and wellness. Thank you."

Order a healing dream when you are going to bed. Say: "Can I have a dream that will help me heal my bones and also bring me feelings of love, joy and happiness. Thank you." Write these words on a piece of paper and put it under your pillow. Go to sleep. Record your dream first thing in the morning.

Emotional release: To complete the process of healing you must work on releasing emotions of anger, resentment, sadness, fear and frustration. Forgive people who hurt you.

Colour therapy: You should work with green, yellow and orange for cleansing and strengthening. Use red to stimulate and energise for bone weakness problems.

Bowels:

The bowels stand for your ability to let go of waste. If you are having problems you have been unable to let go of the old beliefs that you no longer need. Also, you may be feeling judgmental towards others and yourself, being inflexible and wanting everything your way. You may be trying to control others and telling them what they should do with their life. In addition, you are feeling stuck, frustrated and afraid to change things.

Healing Technique:

Bowel problems can result in diarrhea or constipation. In both cases energetic cleansing is a necessity, spend at least 30 minutes a day doing energy cleansing for your bowels.

Here is the cleansing routine.

Take a few slow deep breaths. Tune into your bowels and visualise them. Breathe through them for 3-5 minutes. Ask yourself: "What's holding me back in life? Is there something or someone that I must let go?" Listen to the answer... Don't judge, just acknowledge what you receive.

Rub your hands together for 30 seconds to energise them. Place your hand(s) 6-7 inches above your bowels and sense its energy. Start a downward sweeping motion at the area you wish to treat and visualise you are sweeping away the pain, toxicity and blockages from your bowels. Throw the negative energy in the fire, a candle or an imaginary fire. Repeat the word 'Clear' a few times to strengthen the intention.

Say: "Intuitive Healing Power, please release all pain, negativity and fear from my bowels. Allow me to let go negative beliefs and all points of view that contribute to this condition. Thank you."

To purify your bowels, put your hand a few inches above the bowels and do an anticlockwise motion.

Say: "Intuitive Healing Power, please instil confidence, peace and comfort to my bowels. Allow me to feel safe, secure, supported and protected. Thank you."

Now visualise that your hands are transmitting a yellow light. Transfer the yellow light by doing clockwise movements near the bowels.

Say: "Intuitive Healing Power, please heal my bowels to their maximum health and vitality. Thank you. Thank you. Thank you."

Before going to sleep make a request: "I need a dream that will help me heal my bowels and will make me feel love and joy."

Emotional release: To complete the process of healing you must work on releasing emotions of fear, frustration, rejection and jealousy.

Colour therapy: You should work with yellow, green and orange for cleansing. Work with pink for self-love and self-acceptance.

Brain:

The brain represents your body's computer and switchboard. Your negative thoughts and stresses become your computer's viruses, therefore you must eliminate them. You probably feel out of control, numb, depressed, disinterested, disheartened and tired. You may also feel like you are stuck in an old pattern and your mind is vague, disorganised or conflicted. You're stubbornly refusing to change the way you think.

Healing Technique:

Sit comfortably. Close your eyes and tune into your brain. Consciously relax your scalp and your head. Breathe through your head until you start feeling tingling sensations in your scalp. Spread these sensations to the top of your head, forehead, face, and then go inside of your head. Notice how much clearer your brain is becoming. You should do this technique before studying or taking a test, it helps you to concentrate and utilise your brain power.

Ask yourself: "What mental pattern keeps me stuck? What thoughts and behaviours must I change?" Listen to the answer.

Rub your hands together for 30 seconds or until they tingle. Put your hand(s) a few inches from your forehead and start a downward movement like you're trying to clean the aura of your head. Throw the negative energy in to the fire, a candle or an imaginary one.

Say: "Intuitive Healing Power, I ask you to release stubbornness, negativity and the old mental patterns that keep me stuck. Please make me free from negative thoughts and feelings that are continuously on my mind. Thank you."

To purify your brain do anticlockwise movements with your hand. Start from your forehead and continue to the sides of your head and face. Feel your brain is becoming lighter and clearer.

Say: "Intuitive Healing Power, please instil clarity, trust and peace into my brain. Allow me to become creative, playful and spontaneous. Thank you."

Now imagine your hands are transmitting a purple light. Transfer this purple light to your brain by placing your hands a few inches from your head. Do clockwise movements with your hand(s) to put the energy in.

In order to improve concentration use a violet light, to improve memory use an indigo light.

Say: "Intuitive Healing Power please heal and rejuvenate my brain and bring it to its maximum health and vitality. Thank you."

Ask for a healing dream before going to bed. Say: "I need to experience a healing dream that helps me become a loving operator of my brain. Thank you."

Emotional release: You must release criticism, judgment, control and stubbornness.

Colour therapy: Work with purple, violet and indigo to improve your memory and concentration. Yellow can help you clean the old thoughts and mental patterns also.

Breasts:

The breasts represent feelings of nurturing, gentleness and love. Breast problems occur when you're over mothering others and don't nurture yourself, thinking that others deserve your love more than you do. Neglecting yourself.

Right Breast:

Having too busy a life and not resting yourself. Being a workaholic, inability to say 'no' to others, trying to please everyone, having too many responsibilities and feeling like a slave. Holding on to the victimhood mentality that originates from your childhood and represents the hurts from your family, feeling overpowered by others and trying to control your relationship which can be abusive and chaotic. Carrying a lot of negativity about men and thinking that men caused your problems. Longing for a perfect relationship and feeling jealous to those who have a better relationship then yours.

Left Breast:

Having problems with expressing your femininity, receiving love and affection from others, rejecting help and feeling that you should do everything yourself. Having no clear boundaries and not knowing exactly what you want. Trying to please others in order to be liked, worrying about situations which are outside of your control. Living in constant fear and regretting the choices once made, having a wishy-washy mentality and living in the past.

Healing Technique:

Tune into your breast. Take a few deep breaths and exhale through your breast. Feel the subtle energy inside it. Ask yourself: "Who do I nurture more then I nurture myself?" Listen to the answer...

Stand in front of the mirror and look at your bare breasts. Notice how you feel about them? What is so special about them? Touch them with your hands and feel their texture, shape, temperature etc.

Rub your hands together for 30 seconds to energise them. Place your hand 5-6 inches from your breast and feel the energy of your breast. Make downwards movements with your hand clearing the aura in each of your breasts. Repeat the word 'Clear' a few times to enhance the intention.

Say: "Intuitive Healing Power please release all my guilt, shame, criticism and the feelings of inadequacy from my breasts." Visualise a dark cloud of negative energy leaving your breast.

To purify the energy do anticlockwise movements over each breast. Feel that you are removing all toxicity and negativity. Throw the energetic rubbish into the fire, a candle, or an imaginary fire.

Imagine your hands are transmitting pink rays of light. Transfer pink energy into your breasts by doing clockwise movements over each breast.

Say: "Intuitive Healing Power please instil love, self-respect and self-acceptance into my breasts. Allow me to love myself unconditionally. Thank you."

Bathe your breasts with the pink energy of unconditional love.

Say: "Intuitive Healing Power please heal and rejuvenate my breasts. Allow me to express my femininity and be proud of myself. Thank you, thank you, thank you…"

Give yourself love every day. Say: "I love you" every time you look in a mirror and see your own image. Give yourself compliments. Start and finish your day with the words, "I love you…"

Ask for a healing dream. Say: "I need a dream that helps me heal my breasts and allows me to care and nurture myself." Record your dream first thing in the morning.

Emotional release: To complete the process of healing you must release the feelings of fear, guilt, shame, criticism, judgment, and low self-esteem.

Colour therapy: Use green and orange for clearing the negative energy. Use pink and gold for love and abundance.

Buttocks:

The buttocks connect to your power. Problems in this area mean you're losing your power, feeling unsafe, insecure, unsupported and disappointed with how others treat you. Holding on to negativity, anger and guilt, thinking that you're sexuality unattractive or in a trapped relationship, doubtful about the future, losing your wisdom and not trusting your intuition.

Healing Technique:

If your buttocks are tight consciously try to relax them. Tune into your buttocks and feel the energy inside the muscles. Breathe through them for 2-3 minutes. Visualise that with every exhale you are releasing tension from your buttocks.

Say: "Intuitive Healing Power please remove all guilt, shame and resentment from my buttocks. Allow me to release all negative charge and all points of view that contributed to this problem."

Now, tighten your buttocks and hold the tightness for 5 seconds, then release. Repeat this 10 times. Feel the difference between tightness and relaxation in your buttocks, sense the energy of relaxation.

Rub your hands together for 30 seconds. Spread them slightly apart and visualise the colour silver between your hands. Then, place your hands on your buttocks and visualise bathing them with silver light.

Say: "Intuitive Healing Power please instil strength, power and confidence into my buttocks. Allow me to feel safe and secure. Thank you."

Rub your hands together again and imagine your hands are transmitting a red light. Put your hands on your buttocks and feel the power of the colour red in your buttocks.

Say: "Intuitive Healing Power please rejuvenate my buttocks to their full strength and power. Thank you."

Every day complement yourself and acknowledge your own power, sexiness and vitality. Touch your buttocks and say: "I am safe, secure, supported and protected."

Every night before sleeping, sit on your bed and visualise solid roots coming from your buttocks and going down into the earth, imagine yourself like a tree with strong and powerful roots. Repeat again and again: "I am safe, secure, supported and protected."

Ask for a healing dream at night. Say: "Can I have a dream that helps me restore my power and heals my buttocks. Thank you."

Emotional release: To complete the healing process you must release the feelings of fear, guilt, anger, shame and judgment.

Colour therapy: Use silver for grounding and purification. Use orange for cleansing. Use red for strengthening and empowering.

Cervix:

The cervix symbolises your connection to creativity and femininity. A problem with the cervix means that you are disconnected from your intuitive side and uncomfortable with who you are. You often feel like a victim, unloved, unappreciated and taken for granted, uncomfortable with your femininity. You feel being controlled or in a trapped relationship, longing for love and affection. You can't forgive and let go of the past, you have many regrets and often think, "If only things (this and that) were different."

Healing Technique:

To heal, you need to become comfortable with who you are and embrace your femininity fully. Take a few deep breaths and relax as much as you can. Look at yourself in the mirror and connect with your eyes. Ask yourself, "Where in my life am I denying who I am? How and why do I let others dominate me and run my life for me? In what way am I uncomfortable with being a woman?"

Listen to the answers... Don't judge, just acknowledge what you receive.

Allow your body to soften and relax even more and imagine that you are showered with rays of orange light. Say: "Intuitive Healing Power, I ask you to release all criticism, judgments, resistance and self-righteousness from my body. Please dissolve all feelings of victimhood, fear, ignorance, conflict and manipulation that contributed to this condition. Thank you."

Visualise that orange rays are clearing your body, especially your reproductive system from negative energy. Repeat the word 'Clear' a few times until you feel lighter.

Rub your hands together for 30 seconds until they tingle. Start with a downward sweeping motion at your lower abdomen. Visualise sweeping away all negativity from your reproductive system. To purify the energy start an anticlockwise movement with your hand. Feel lighter and clearer.

Say: "Intuitive Healing Power, please instil the feelings of love and kindness into my reproductive system. Allow me to love myself and express my femininity with ease. Thank you."

Breathe deeply through your lower abdomen and when you exhale say, "Haaaaaaaaaaaaaaaaaaa." Feel the vibration of the sound in your belly. Repeat this 7 times. The vibration of this sound helps to stimulate your cervix to heal it.

Say: "Intuitive Healing Power, please heal my cervix to its maximum health and vitality. Please restore my health and strengthen my mind and spirit. Thank you."

Ask for a healing dream. Say: "Intuitive Healing Power, I need a dream that helps me heal my cervix and restore my femininity."

Emotional release: To complete the healing process you must release the feelings of fear, grief anger, shame and criticism.

Colour therapy: Use orange, green and yellow for cleansing. Use pink to instil unconditional love. Use gold for abundance.

Chest:

The chest is your emotional storage point. Pains and aches show that you are burdened by your past experiences and carrying too much emotional baggage such as unexpressed emotions. You are giving away your energy to others and not getting anything in return, you are trying to control situations and people that seem uncontrollable. You are unable to say "no" and are doing things just to please others.

Healing Technique:

The chest represents your capacity to breathe and feel free. Unexpressed emotions make the chest congested, therefore, energy cleansing must become your necessary daily routine.

Sit comfortably. Tune into your chest by focusing on your breath. Breathe deeply and slowly. Visualise the inside of your chest.

Rub your hands together for 30 seconds to energise them. Place your hand 5-6 inches above your chest, sense the energy and then start a downward sweeping movement over the area. Visualise you are sweeping away all density, negativity and irritation. Throw the negative energy in the fire, a candle or an imaginary fire. Repeat the word 'Clear' a few times to strengthen the intention. Continue sweeping for 5-10 min or until you feel lighter.

Say: "Intuitive Healing Power, please remove all burdens, stress, infection and toxins from my chest. Allow me to breathe freely. Thank you"

Visualise your hands are transmitting a bright orange light which is the best colour for rapid cleaning of the airways. Place your hand(s) 5-6 inches from your chest and do an anticlockwise motion to purify your chest with orange light.

Continue for 5 minutes or until you feel lighter.

Say: "Intuitive Healing Power, please instill lightness, freedom, and openness into my chest. Allow me to feel loving and confident and assist me to live my life from the heart. Thank you."

Continue bathing your chest with orange colour but now start clockwise movement with your hand to put the energy in. Say: "Intuitive Healing Power, please heal and rejuvenate my chest to the maximum health, vitality and wellbeing. Thank you."

Before going to sleep ask for a healing dream. Say: "I need a dream which helps me heal my chest and brings peace and relaxation into my life." Write it on a piece of paper and put this paper under your pillow. Record your dream in the morning.

Emotional release: To complete the process of healing you must work on releasing overwhelming sadness, control, frustration and low self-esteem. Forgiveness is necessary to heal this problem.

Colour therapy: You should work with green, yellow and orange to clean and strengthen the system. Use pink to instil more love.

Ears:

Problems with the ears imply that you don't like what you hear. You probably feel stuck in a situation or are angry with it. You hold on to blame, criticism and resentment, hearing wrong things and misunderstanding what you hear. You are stubborn and refusing to change.

Right Ear:

Experiencing a lot of conflict, feeling impatient and angry with others and don't want to listen. You can't let go of destructive beliefs from the past, feeling exhausted in regards to your environment and people close to you.

Left Ear:

Low self-esteem. Criticising yourself and thinking you're not important. Feeling that people don't like you and dominate you. Wanting to find the way out of the situation you are in.

Healing Technique:

There is so much noise around you that you don't like to hear and your ears absorb negativity like a sponge. To heal you must become aware of which noises cause you damage and what makes you block your awareness.

Sit comfortably, take a few slow breaths and ask yourself: "What kind of things don't I like to hear? Where do these sounds come from?"

Listen to the answer... Don't judge, just receive a message.

Tune into your ears. Sense the subtle energy inside them. Rub your hands together for 30 seconds to energise them. Put your right hand a few inches from your right ear and your left hand at your left ear. Start a downwards movement. Imagine you are clearing away all negativity and toxicity. Throw the energetic toxins into a fire, a candle or an imaginary fire.

Repeat the word 'Clear' a few times to enhance the clearing process.

Say: "Intuitive Healing Power, please remove all negativity, criticism, guilt, anger and resentment from my ears. Please eliminate all energy, negative and positive as well as all points of view that contribute to this condition. Thank you."

To purify the energy around your ears do an anticlockwise movement with your hands. Imagine your hands are transmitting a purple light. Purple is the healing colour for hearing. Put your hands close to your ears and bathe your ears in purple.

Say: "Intuitive Healing Power, please allow me to clear my hearing and experience harmony, peace, and balance in my life. Thank you."

Take a few deep slow breaths and listen to your breathing.

Say: "Intuitive Healing Power, please heal my ears and restore my hearing abilities to their maximum level. Thank you."

Ask for a healing dream before going to bed. Say: "I need a dream to help me heal my ears and make me experience peace and trust."

Emotional release: To complete the process of healing you must work on releasing emotions of anger, feeling stuck, criticism, frustration and low self-esteem.

Colour therapy: You should work with purple, mauve and violet for better hearing.

Elbows:

Elbow disease implies that you are losing your directions in life, becoming stubborn, inflexible, stagnant, limited, frustrated and disconnected from your intuition. You are not in touch with your body's needs and believe that you must struggle to survive. You focus on others but ignore yourself.

Right Elbow:

Not trusting and feeling let down by others, you are holding onto many hurts and much anger, and are not able to forgive or let go.

Left Elbow:

Feeling weak, unsupported, stressed and overwhelmed, you have no personal power and do not believe in yourself. You can't make your own decisions, and you have a lot of suppressed anger and frustrations.

Healing Technique:

Tune into your elbow. Feel the sensations inside the joint. Breathe through the pain and discomfort. Listen to the pain. If the elbow pain was an object, what would it be? (A splinter or a nail ...) Is the pain sharp or dull? What colour is it? Is it warm or cold?

Breathe slowly and deeply and synchronise with your pain. Every time you exhale visualise that the pain is being expelled from your elbow.

Say: "Intuitive Healing Power, please dissolve all pain, stiffness, struggle, weakness, rigidity and anger from my elbow. Thank you."

Rub your hands together for 30 seconds to energise them. Put your right hand a few inches from your left elbow and start a downward sweeping movement. Visualise you are sweeping away all the pain and negativity. Throw the negative energy into the fire, a candle or an imaginary fire. Repeat the word 'Clear' a few times to strengthen the intention.

Say: "Intuitive Healing Power, please instil flexibility, ease and grace into my elbow and into my body. Thank you."

Visualise your hands are transmitting green light. Transfer this healing light to your elbow by doing clockwise movements over the joint.

Say: "Intuitive Healing Power, please heal and regenerate my elbow to its maximum health and strength. Thank you."

Do the same process with the other elbow.

Before going to bed say: "I need to experience a dream that helps me heal my elbow and put me into the flow of life." Write it down on a piece of paper and put it under your pillow. Record your dream first thing in the morning.

Emotional release: To complete the process of healing you must work on releasing emotions of anger, frustration and jealousy.

Colour therapy: You should work with green and yellow for cleaning the energy. Work with silver for getting clarity and dissolving confusion.

Eyes:

Eye problems connect to feelings of not liking what you see in your environment. You may be feeling stuck and seeing things from one side only, refusing to see others points of view. You are focusing on obstacles and limitations and having fears about the future. Children with eye problems don't want to see their parents fight and argue.

Right Eye:

Sabotaging yourself and blocking the flow of abundance. You are holding onto old pains from past relationships with others, not seeing the solution to improve your situation, and focusing on why things don't work and making excuses. You feel irritated and angry with yourself and others.

Left Eye:

Feeling victimised and disconnected from your intuition and creativity. You are seeing everything from a negative point of view, and holding on to stress, worry and fear. You are experiencing a lack of joy, spontaneity and creativity.

Healing Technique:

Close your eyes and relax. Tune into your eyes. What can you sense there? Ask yourself: "What are the things that I don't want to see? Who are the people around me that I don't like to see? What are the situations that make me feel bad?"

Listen to the answers...

If you want to heal your eyes you need to stop focusing on what you don't want to see and start focusing on positive things in your life. You must start seeing the beauty and relate to joy in order to heal.

Connect to nature, go for a bush walk, sit on a beach and watch the waves, the sun and the water birds. Go to a gallery and look at the beautiful paintings. Enjoy the beauty of the flowers in the garden. Seeing this beauty helps to restore your vision.

When you are outside, sense the energy in your eyes and say: "Intuitive Healing Power, please release all negativity, suspicion and criticism from my eyes. Help me to see the beauty and vibrancy of nature. Thank you."

Rub your hands together for 30 seconds or until they are warm. Hold them apart and visualise a purple light between them. Close your eyes and gently place your hands on your eyes. Avoid applying pressure to your eyeballs. Bathe your eyes with purple and sense the colour.

Say: "Intuitive Healing Power, please instil clarity, trust, patience and relaxation into my eyes. Thank you."

Roll your eyes clockwise, then anti-clockwise. Repeat 5 times. Open your eyes and focus on a distant object for 10-15 seconds. Then, slowly refocus your eyes on a nearby object without moving your head. Do this 5 times and then relax your eyes.

Say: "Intuitive Healing Power, please heal and rejuvenate my vision to its maximum health and wellness. Thank you."

Before going to sleep ask: "I need a dream that helps to heal my eyes and restore my capacity to see with love and joy. Thank you."

Emotional release: To complete the process of healing you must work on releasing emotions of fear, stress, frustration and jealousy. Work on forgiveness.

Colour therapy: You should work with indigo, purple, blue, violet and mauve to restore your vision and heal your eyes.

Face:

The face constitutes your self-expression and what you show to the world. Face disease implies that you are losing your face by repeating the same mistakes. You are not following your intuition, acting against your heart, and holding onto limiting beliefs, struggle, stress and fears. You are not loving yourself and wearing a mask to hide behind it.

Healing Technique:

Look in the mirror and touch your face. Touch your cheeks, nose, forehead and chin. Acknowledge all the parts you like and the parts you don't like about your face. Think about why you don't like them. Do they remain you of the mask you're wearing that you hide behind? What are these situations you can't face and are hiding from? Are these the people you need to confront? Are there projects that you want to start but procrastinate? Take notice of the answers and start taking steps towards facing all these situations.

Now spend a few minutes massaging your face with an oil or cream. Then close your eyes, take a deep breath in and out and say out loud, "I love you ….(say your name)." Repeat this 5 times and make sure you say it from the heart.

Rub your hands together for 30 seconds until they feel warm. Put your hand(s) a few inches from your face and start a downward movement like you are trying to remove the mask. Throw the energy of the mask into a fire, light a candle or an imaginary fire.

Say: "Intuitive Healing Power, please help me remove the mask, strain, stress and struggles from my face. Thank you."

Repeat the word 'Clear' a few times to strengthen the intention.

Visualise your hands are transmitting an orange energy. Put your hands over your face and bathe it with orange light, sense its energy.

Say: "Intuitive Healing Power, please instil courage, confidence and inner strength into my face. Allow me to connect with spirit and intuition. Thank you."

Breathe through your face until you sense a tingling. If you have facial paralysis you should do this for 30 minutes every day.

Say: "Intuitive Healing Power, please heal and regenerate my face to its maximum health, vigour and beauty. Thank you."

When going to bed ask for a healing dream. Say: "I need a dream that helps me to express who I am and helps me face my life with strength and courage. Thank you."

Emotional release: To complete the process of healing you must work on releasing the emotions of fear, rejection, stress, frustration and jealousy. Work on forgiveness.

Colour therapy: You should work with orange, purple and pink.

Fallopian Tubes:

The fallopian tubes symbolise your connection to the creative side of life. If you have problems, you are feeling stuck and lost, carrying sadness and shame in regards to femininity and having children. You are suppressing joy, self-expression and sensuality; having difficulty moving forward and finding your way.

Healing Technique:

Visualise your fallopian tubes. Tune into them. Feel the energy inside and ask yourself: "In what way do I deny my femininity? How do I sabotage my ability to have healthy children? Where do my limited beliefs about sexuality and sensuality come from?"

Listen to the answers, don't judge them, just receive and take notice. Answering these questions helps you to release stagnant and stuck energy in regards to your reproductive organs.

Rub your hands together for 30 seconds to energise them. Put your hands over your fallopian tubes and sense the energy they transmit. Start a downward sweeping motion at this area. Visualise you are sweeping away all negativity and blockages from your fallopian tubes. Repeat the word 'Clear' a few times to strengthen the intention. Continue sweeping for 5-10 minutes or until you feel lighter.

Say: "Intuitive Healing Power, please remove all guilt, shame, loneliness, grief, depression and feelings of loss from my reproductive organs. Please release all negative points of view that contribute to this condition. Thank you."

Rub your hands together and imagine they are transmitting a bright orange light. Place your hands over your fallopian tubes and start a clockwise movement. Visualise an orange light moving into your fallopian tubes, dissolving all blockages and energising them.

Say: "Intuitive Healing Power, please energise my fallopian tubes and help me express my femininity freely. Please connect me to my intuition, creativity and bring back my sense of youth, vibrancy and vitality. Thank you."

Repeat the same process with a pink light.

Say: "Intuitive Healing Power, please heal and regenerate my fallopian tubes and all reproductive organs to their maximum health and wellness. Thank you."

Before going to bed say: "Intuitive Healing Power, I need a guidance dream to restore my femininity, creativity and the health of my reproductive system. Thank you."

Emotional release: To complete the process of healing you must work on releasing emotions of fear, sadness, resentment, shame, frustration and jealousy. Forgiveness is necessary.

Colour therapy: You should work with orange and yellow to clean the negativity from your fallopian tubes. Use pink for love and forgiveness.

Feet:

The feet represent your directions in life. A problematic foot means that you are probably stuck in a pattern of moving in the wrong direction, not listening to your inner voice and feeling obligated to others.

You are probably unhappy with what you've got and wanting to be in a different place.

Right Foot:

Focusing on the material world and ignoring the spirit. Forcing things to happen rather than letting them unfold by themselves. You are holding onto stress, obligation, frustration and disappointments, and feeling disconnected from the natural flow of life. You are sabotaging yourself.

Left Foot:

Trying to please others. Feeling hurt in personal relationships. Not knowing what you want out of life. You have difficulty finding a new direction, you think that you never got what you wanted and you are blaming yourself and others.

Healing Technique:

Feet problems should make you think of your direction in life. Ask yourself: "What is stopping me from moving in the direction I want? What am I afraid of? Where do I sabotage myself? Do I allow others to sabotage me?"

To heal your feet you need to be able to let go the past and start moving into the future with confidence.

Your feet carry you around, they do such a great job for you, your job is to love and appreciate your feet. Start connecting to your feet by massaging them daily. A great way to start a foot massage is to soak your feet in a bowl of warm, scented water. Fill a large bowl with warm water and add a couple of drops of your favourite essential oil, (lavender and peppermint are excellent). Put your feet in and luxuriate for as long as you like before starting the foot massage. You can start by massaging the middle of your foot first, then massage the heel, the outer sides and the ball of your foot. Separately massage each toe. When massaging your feet think loving thoughts about your feet, they deserve your love.

Feet connect us to the Earth. We can ground ourselves through our feet and release negative and dense energy into the ground.

Now, stand straight and put your feet shoulder width apart. Imagine that there are two big tubes going through your feet and connecting you to the ground. Visualise that you are releasing negative energy into the ground through these tubes. Feel the lightness.

Say: "Intuitive Healing Power, please release all negativity, burdens, limitations, anger, frustration and neglect from my feet. Help me remove all negative charge and all points of view that contribute to this problem. Thank you."

Now, visualise the colour of Earth's energy streaming up from the ground into your feet and into your body. Feel strong and confident.

Say: "Intuitive Healing Power, please instil strength, confidence and the ability to move forward into my body. Let me keep my feet on the ground and follow my own intuitive guidance. Allow me to feel happy, joyful and powerful. Thank you."

Breathe through your feet for a few minutes. Sense the energy inside your feet.

Say: "Intuitive Healing Power, please heal and regenerate my feet to their maximum health and strength. Thank you."

Emotional release: To complete the process of healing you must work on releasing emotions of anger, sadness, resentment, hurt, frustration and feelings of being stuck.

Colour therapy: You should work with green for cleansing, pink to instil love and red for getting your power back. Use brown for grounding.

Fingers:

The fingers represent the details of life as well as your ability to touch, hold, give and receive. Fingers correspond with the five energy centres: the Root chakra, Sacral chakra, Solar Plexus, Heart and Throat chakras.

Thumb:

The thumb is connected to your head, intellect, self-will and motivations. It holds powerful energies of creativity, sexual expression and drive. Thumb problems represent feeling weak, lost and disturbed. A healthy thumb helps to bring balance in life.

Index Finger:

The index finger is connected to your self-love, feeling of security and how you think about yourself and the life around you. It represents your connection to power. If you have problems with it, you may suffer from control problems, you may try to control others or feel that they control you.

Middle Finger:

The middle finger is connected to your personal power, stamina, sexuality, sensuality and your ability to deal with life challenges. Middle finger problems imply that you feel uncomfortable with your weight and sexuality. You may hold a lot of unexpressed anger inside.

Ring Finger:

The ring finger is connected to how you feel about other people, especially your family and partners. If you have problems with your ring finger you may feel unloved, rejected and not nurtured. Your ability to give and receive love is compromised.

Little Finger:

The little finger is connected to your feelings about your family and tribe. What do you feel about them? Do you like them? Do you feel proud to be a part of your tribe? Problems with the little finger imply that you feel insecure, unsafe, unsupported and/or rejected. You may feel not good enough, not strong enough, not courageous enough.

Healing Technique:

To heal a finger you must restore balance in the area of life which the finger represents. Close your eyes. Focus on your finger and ask: "What is the message you are trying to send me?" Listen to the answer...

Rub your hands together until they're warm. Using the fingers on the other hand remove the negative energy from each finger. Gently pull each finger and visualise you are pulling off blockages, toxicity, dullness and stress. Say: "Intuitive Healing Power, help me release all negativity and density from my fingers. Help me restore balance in my life. Thank you."

Throw the negative energy into a fire. you should light a candle for this.

Gently massage your fingers. Start massaging from the base of each finger and go up towards the points.

You can use colours to energise and rejuvenate your fingers, because fingers correspond with different chakras, you should use a certain colour for each finger.

> For the thumb it is a blue colour
> For the index finger it is a green colour
> For the middle finger it is a yellow colour
> For the ring finger it is an orange colour
> For the little finger it is a red colour

Visualise your hand is transmitting a colour. Wrap your hand around the finger on the other hand and bathe it with this colour. Say: "Intuitive Healing Power, please help to heal and rejuvenate my finger to its maximum health and vitality. Thank you."

You can also work with the corresponding chakra for that finger. You can clean and energise the chakra for the best results.

Ask for a healing dream. Say: "I need intuitive guidance on how to heal my fingers. Thank you."

Emotional release: To complete the process of healing you must work on releasing emotions that correspond with the finger.

Colour therapy: You should work with the colour that corresponds with the finger.

Gall bladder:

The gall bladder is a container of your negative emotions especially unexpressed anger and resentment. Disease of the gall bladder is also connected to grieving about men or processing unresolved male energy. You probably have too much pride to admit your mistakes and talk to people about your conflicts; you struggle to achieve things by feeling that you are not good enough to get to the top of things. You may also sabotage yourvself saying words like, "I would love to do (or have) this, BUT...."

Healing Technique:

Tune into your gall bladder. Look up the structure of the organ to see and visualise it clearly. Imagine your gall bladder is a bag that stores negativity and blockages. Ask yourself: "What feelings do I keep inside that have contributed to this condition? In what way do I sabotage myself? "

Listen to the answer...

With your mind's eye look at your gall bladder and describe it, what colour is it? Is it empty or full? What shape is it?

If your gall bladder is full, imagine you're empting the content. If it's red and inflamed visualise dissolving the redness.

Now, rub your hands together until they are warm. Put your right hand a few inches from the gall bladder area and feel the energy generated by your gall bladder. Start doing a downward sweeping movement in this area. Visualise you're sweeping away the toxins and negativity.

Say: "Intuitive Healing Power, please release all anger, resentment, grief, self-sabotage and confusion from my system as well as all negative charge and all points of view that contributed to this condition. Thank you."

Repeat the word 'Clear' a few times to make the intention stronger.

Visualise your hands are transmitting a green light. Put your hands closer to your gall bladder and bathe the organ with green. Start a clockwise movement with your hands over the area to put the green energy into your gall bladder.

Say: "Intuitive Healing Power, please instil clarity, confidence and satisfaction into my system. Allow me to experience grace and ease. Thank you."

Keep doing the circular movements with your hand(s) and repeat the words, "Heal. Purify. Restore." Visualise your gallbladder in its pristine condition.

Say: "Intuitive Healing Power, please heal and rejuvenate my gall bladder and the related organs to their maximum health and wellness. Thank you. "

Before going to bed, ask for a healing dream. Say: "I need to experience a dream that brings me joy, sweetness and healing. Thank you." Keep your attention on your gall bladder when you're trying to fall asleep.

Emotional release: To complete the process of healing you must work on releasing emotions such as sadness, anger, rejection, criticism and grief.

Colour therapy: You should work with green, yellow and orange.

Gums:

The gums symbolise your ability to speak for yourself, chew and bite. Problems here imply that you have a wishy-washy mentality, unable to back up your decisions, experience lack of confidence, procrastinating, giving up on your dreams as well as feeling insecure and fearful to express yourself.

Healing Technique:

Tune into your gums. Feel the energy inside as a tingling sensation. Ask yourself: "Where in life do I feel insecure and can't speak for myself? What am I afraid of? " Listen to the answer...

Rub your hands together for 30 seconds. Place your hand(s) near your gums and start a downward sweeping motion. Visualise cleaning your gums and throw the bad stuff into a fire, a candle or an imaginary fire.

Say: "Intuitive Healing Power, please release insecurity, self-sabotage and stagnation from my gums. Help me release all points of views that contributed to this condition. Thank you."

Visualise your hands are transmitting an orange light. Put your hands closer to your mouth and bathe your gums in the orange colour.

Say: "Intuitive Healing Power, please instil courage, confidence and the ability to speak for myself into my gums. Allow me to express myself freely and easily. Thank you."

Massage your gums with your finger and baking soda. Baking soda neutralises acid, kills bacteria and prevents decay. Mix a teaspoon of baking soda and a teaspoon of water in a small cup. Stir the solution. Massage your entire gum line with the baking soda solution beginning from the front to the sides of the mouth. Massage for 30 seconds each side, then rinse your mouth with fresh water.

Visualise white rays of purifications spreading through your gums while massaging them.

Say: "Intuitive Healing Power, please heal and regenerate my gums to their maximum health and allow me to feel secure, confident and positive. Thank you."

At night ask for a healing dream. Say: "Can I experience a dream that helps me speak the truth with ease and grace and heal my gums at the same time. Thank you."

Emotional release: To complete the process of healing you must work on releasing emotions of fear, anger, rejection, criticism and the feeling of being stuck.

Colour therapy: You should work with white and green for purification. Use orange and red for stimulation and growth.

Hair:

Your hair represents beauty, strength, freedom and power. Problems occur when you experience worry, stress, tension, thinking too much and feel disconnected and lost. You may also be pushing things forcefully rather than letting them unfold naturally.

Healing Technique:

Tune into your scalp. What sensations do you feel? Acknowledge your feelings.

Rub your hands together for 30 seconds to energise them. Start massaging your scalp. Visualise a green light coming from your fingers while massaging your scalp. Begin massaging from the top of your head to the sides.

Say: "Intuitive Healing Power, please remove all stress, worries, fears, frustrations and tension from my scalp. Allow me to release all negative points of view that contribute to this condition. Thank you."

Repeat the word 'Clear' a few times to make the intention stronger.

Focus on each part of your scalp separately: The top, the sides and the lower scalp. Sense the energy in each part and bathe it in a green colour.

Imagine the hair roots are becoming stronger and more vital. To improve blood circulation in the roots of your hair visualise the colour red spreading inside your scalp.

Say: "Intuitive Healing Power please heal and regenerate my hair and scalp to its maximum health and vitality. Thank you."

At night, ask for a healing dream. Say: "Intuitive Healing Power, please give me guidance on how to restore my beauty and my confidence. Thank you." Focus on your hair and scalp when trying to fall asleep.

Emotional release: To complete the process of healing you must work on releasing emotions such as stress, fear, anger, rejection, criticism and guilt.

Colour therapy: You should work with white and green for cleaning and purification. Use the colour red for hair growth stimulation.

Hands:

The hands represent your ability to hold and handle things. If you have problems with your hands you experience fear, hold onto old and outdated beliefs and reject new ones. Your worries and criticisms contribute to creating an arthritic hand. Or you may be trying to help everybody but forget to help yourself which creates a 'helping' hand.

Right Hand:

If your right hand is your dominant hand you may feel that you have lost the ability to create. You feel disappointed, betrayed and rejected, afraid of your ability to make money and feed your family. You may have problems with male members of your family or difficulty managing masculine power.

Left Hand:

Holding onto old hurts related to the female side of your family. Feeling lonely and isolated, not having clear directions in life. Shifting your responsibility to someone else rather than become strong and empowered. Resisting life, not knowing how to take care of yourself.

Healing Technique:

Your hands are your healing tool. Hands have the ability to generate and sense energy. Rub your hands together for 30 seconds to generate a natural healing energy. Have them slightly apart and sense the energy. Say: "I am activating my healing energy now."

Imagine a green light comes from the palms of your hands. Visualise the green energy penetrates through the skin, muscles and bones of your hands.

Say: "Intuitive Healing Power please release all stress, resistance, criticism, blame, hurt and tension as well as all points of view that contribute to this problem. Thank you."

Massage each hand with the other hand, and pull negative energy from each hand as if you're removing gloves from your hands. Throw the negative energy into a fire and burn it. Light a candle or imagine a fire.

Repeat the word 'Clear' a few times to strengthen the healing intention.

Clasp your hands together interlocking your fingers. Imagine a gold light penetrates your hands and is moving through your hands.

Say: "Intuitive Healing Power please instil strength, confidence, clarity, patience and power into my system. Make me handle all things with ease and grace. Thank you. "

Sense the gold light vibrations inside both hands.

Say: "Intuitive Healing Power please heal and rejuvenate my hands to their maximum health and strength. Thank you."

Before going to sleep ask for a healing dream. Say: "Can I have a dream that helps me heal my hands and also makes me feel loving, joyful and strong. Thank you."

Emotional release: To complete the process of healing you must work on releasing control, stress, fear, criticism and the feeling of being stuck.

Colour therapy: You should work with white and green for cleaning and purification. Use gold and pink for love and strength.

Head:

The head represents your capacity to process your thoughts and emotions. Problems imply that you experience fear, tension, uncertainty and refuse to accept what's going on. You criticise yourself and others, try to control people and situations, strive to be perfect and self- righteous and are burdened by too many responsibilities.

Healing Technique:

Tune into your head. Breathe deeply and slowly. When exhaling, push the air through your head. Imagine it gets lighter with every breath. With your mind's eye look inside your head: What do you see? Is the place looking dull or bright? Is it empty or congested? Is it warm or cold? Does it feel hard or soft?

Rub your hands together for 30 seconds. Move your hands slightly apart and sense the energy. Add in an indigo colour to this energy. Indigo calms, relaxes and relieves headaches.

Then, place your hands on the sides of your head and start massaging your temples with your fingers. Imagine transferring the indigo light into your head.

Say: "Intuitive Healing Power please remove tension, upset, fear and stubbornness from my head. Thank you."

Massage the area around your eyes and your forehead. Imagine an indigo light penetrating inside your head and clearing your thoughts and mental chatter. Repeat the word 'Clear' a few times to strengthen the intention.

Gently stroke your cheeks, temples, forehead and the top of your head trying to relax every muscle around your skull.

Say: "Intuitive Healing Power please instil lightness, clarity and flexibility into my head. Thank you."

Breathe through your head. Sense how the energy changes with your every breath in and out.

Say: "Intuitive Healing Power please heal and rejuvenate my head to its maximum health and brightness. Thank you."

Before going to bed meditate for 5-10 minutes and then say: "I need a dream that can bring peace, relaxation and clarity into my head. Thank you."

Emotional release: To complete the process of healing your head, you must release the feelings of control, judgment, stress, feelings of being overwhelmed and worry.

Colour therapy: You should work with a white light for cleaning and purification. Use indigo to relieve headaches. Use yellow for mental stimulation.

Heart:

The heart represents your ability to love and feel emotionally secure. Heart problems show that you are suffering from a broken heart and long standing emotional problems due to blocking intimacy in your relationship. You may feel angry, disappointed, lonely and taking on too much responsibility for yourself. You envy others regarding their success and achievements.

Healing Technique:

Close your eyes and tune into your heart. Visualise it. Talk to your heart, ask, "Is my heart happy? Where do I block love and intimacy in my relationship? Why is my heart broken?" Listen to the answers. Don't judge, just receive and acknowledge them.

Rub your hands together for 30 seconds. Put your hand(s) a few inches from the middle of your chest and sense the energy your heart emits. Start a downward sweeping motion at this spot. Visualise you are sweeping away all the negative energy. Say: "Intuitive Healing Power, please release all pain, negativity, struggle and blockages from my heart. Thank you." Throw the negative energy into the fire, a candle, or an imaginary fire.

Repeat the word 'Clear' a few times to make your intentions stronger. Continue with the downward sweeping for 3-4 minutes or until you feel lighter.

To purify the energy of your heart do an anticlockwise movement around the heart area for a few minutes.

Then visualise that your hands are transmitting a green light. Place your hands on your chest and transfer this green light into your heart. Do clockwise movements with your hands to move the energy in.

Say: "Intuitive Healing Power, please heal and rejuvenate my heart and related organs to their maximum health and wellness. Thank you."

Always remember that the true essence of the heart is love and joy. If you don't experience love and joy, you are living in your old wounds, you should release your wounds in order to live from the heart, forgiveness is the only way to do that. The act of forgiveness is therapeutic and very powerful, but it has to be done in a correct way. True forgiveness is letting go of all hurtful feelings, sensations and thoughts about the person and the situation caused by that person. This means that when you think about the person or situation you feel just fine, neutral or even light (because you've learned a lesson).

Some people say that they forgave but continue to feel resentment or upset – this means they haven't truly forgiven yet and they need to work more on the process of forgiveness. True forgiveness can improve the health condition of a person on its own; it will heal your heart and improve your health. Refer to the chapter, "How to Forgive."

Before going to bed ask for a healing dream. Say: "I need to experience a dream that will help me truly forgive, and fill my heart with love, joy and peace. Thank you." Write this request on a piece of paper and put it under your pillow. Go to sleep focusing on your hearts energy.

Emotional release: To complete the process of healing your heart you must release sadness, judgment, jealousy, control, stress, fear, criticism and the feelings of being stuck. Forgiveness is necessary to heal.

Colour therapy: You should work with green for cleansing. Use gold and pink for love and abundance.

Heels:

The heels represent strength and grounding. If you have problems with your heels you are feeling confused, vulnerable, doubtful and weak. You avoid dealing directly with problems and tiptoe around others.

Healing Technique:

A heel problem implies you must stop and re-evaluate your life, ask yourself: "Who am I? What am I doing with my life? What do I truly believe in? What does my heart say?" To heal you need to regain your strength and confidence. Answering these questions will help you release the blocked energy and make you feel lighter.

Now, sit comfortably, breathe deeply and slowly. Tune into your heel and feel its energy for a few minutes.

Lift your foot up and place your hand over your toes. Keep your leg steady and pull your foot towards you so the sole of your foot is stretched. Hold this position for approximately 30 seconds and relax. Repeat this stretching 5 times. Visualise that all the negative energy is being released every time you relax your foot. Say: "Intuitive Healing Power please remove all doubt, stress, pain, confusion, weakness and indecisiveness from my heel. Release all negative charge and all points of view that contribute to this condition. Thank you."

Take your socks off and massage your heel. Repeat the word 'Clear' a few times and visualise removing all the pain from your heel.

Imagine your hands are transmitting orange energy. Place your hand on your heel and bathe it in the orange light.

Say: "Intuitive Healing Power please instil confidence, strength, courage and love into my system. Thank you."

If you have plantar fasciitis, (inflammation of the heel tendons), use ice to massage your heel. Just take a piece of ice and perform circular movements over your heel.

Say: "Intuitive Healing Power please heal and rejuvenate my heels to their maximum health and vitality. Thank you."

Ask for a healing dream. Say: "I need to experience a dream to help me become confident and strong and help me to start moving in the direction of my heart desires. Thank you."

Emotional release: To complete the process of healing you must work on releasing fear, stress and low self-esteem.

Colour therapy: You should work with green for cleansing, pink for love and brown for grounding.

Hips:

The hips symbolise your tribal or family connections. Hip problems indicate carrying relationship burdens on your hips and also sexuality and self-expression problems. You do not trust the flow of life and feeling unappreciated, betrayed, deceived, let down and alienated. You are letting others manipulate and take advantage of you, focusing on strain, lack of things, guilt and shame.

Healing Technique:

The hips are the basis of your body. They hold your body and physically support it. That's why the hips correspond with the fundamental issues such as family and trust.

Now tune into your hips. Ask yourself: "What burdens do I carry on my hips? Who do I feed with my energy without getting anything in return?"

Answering these questions will help you release dense and blocked energy from your hips.

Stand up, if you can, and shake your hips. Imagine shaking off all negative energy and problems. If you can't stand up, massage your hips.

Rub your hands together for 30 seconds until they are warm. Put your hands over your hips without touching them and sense the energy. Start a downward sweeping movement. Visualise you're removing toxic energy from your hips.

Say: "Intuitive Healing Power please remove all pain, hardship and negativity from my hips. Please release all anger, victimhood and betrayal from my hips. Thank you." Visualise a dark cloud leaving your hips. Repeat the word 'Clear' a few times to strengthen the intention.

Imagine your hands are transmitting orange lights, (orange is the colour for rapid cleaning and dissolving negative matter). Put your hands on your hips and transfer the orange light deep inside your hips, feel the orange vibrations inside your cells.

Say: "Intuitive Healing Power please energise my hips with confidence, vitality, support and joy. Let me experience harmony, love and happiness. Thank you."

Now imagine your hands are transmitting green light. Green is healing, supporting and a rejuvenating colour. Transfer the green light to your hips, feel the green vibrations inside your hips.

Say: "Intuitive Healing Power please heal and rejuvenate my hips to their maximum health and mobility. Thank you."

Before going to bed ask for a healing dream. Say: "I need to experience a dream that helps me heal and become strong, confident and joyful. Thank you." Focus on your hips while trying to fall asleep.

Emotional release: To complete the process of healing you must work on releasing fear, criticism, judgment, frustration and stress.

Colour therapy: You should work with orange and green for cleaning and rejuvenation. Use pink and gold for love and abundance.

Immune system:

The function of immune system is to protect you from foreign objects. It starts to break down when you experience inner conflict, doubt, irritation and anger. It deteriorates when you are forcing things to happen instead of allowing them to happen, when you are feeling unloved, neglected and thinking that you never get what you want in life and that other people take advantage of you. The immune system can malfunction when you feel overwhelmed, insecure and struggling with life.

Healing Technique:

Sit comfortably. Tune into the centre of your body and breathe deeply. Feel your subtle body energy. Ask yourself: "What burdens am I carrying? What am I struggling with? What beliefs do I hold on to that no longer serve me?" Acknowledge the answers.

Keep focusing on your breath and when you exhale visualise releasing the problems.

Say: "Intuitive Healing Power please remove all baggage, stress, insecurity, shame, guilt and resistance from my system. Help me release all points of view that contribute to this condition. Thank you."

Repeat the word 'Clear' a few times to strengthen the intention.

Visualise an orange light moving into your body, entering from the top of your head and spreading inside. Bathe your whole body with orange energy and sense its vibrations in every cell. Notice how you feel, some parts of your body may start to feel more alive now.

Say: "Intuitive Healing Power please instil joy, happiness and creativity into my body. Allow me to experience love, confidence and freedom. Thank you. "

Experience this vibrational state for at least 15 minutes every day. Make sure to let go all mental chatter while doing this healing technique.

Order a healing dream before going to bed. Say: "I need to experience a dream to help me heal my immune system and make me feel loved, strong and secure." Write these words on a piece of paper and put it under your pillow. Go to sleep.

When you wake up write your dream in a journal, notice the most vivid signs, symbols and emotions.

Emotional release: To complete the healing process on releasing stress, guilt, rejection, shame, fear and frustration, go through a forgiveness process and forgive everyone who contributed to the problem.

Colour therapy: You should work with orange, green, and gold to stimulate your immune system.

Jaw:

The jaw symbolises your capacity to bite. When you have problems with the jaw it means that you are holding on to rage, anger, and resentment. You probably think about revenge but try to suppress your feelings. You may also feel inferior and have difficulty moving forward.

Healing Technique:

Tune into your jaw. Sense the energy inside it and ask yourself, "What feelings do I suppress? Who do I resent? Who and what makes me feel angry?" Become aware of your feelings.

Rub your hands together for 30 seconds. Put your hand over your jaw without touching it and sense its energy. Start a downward sweeping motion as if you're cleaning all the negative energy from it. Visualise removing pain, density and toxicity from your jaw. Burn the negative energy in the fire, a candle or an imaginary fire.

Say: "Intuitive Healing Power please remove all stress, tension, hardship, judgments, criticism and limitations from my jaw. Please release all points of view and all charge, positive and negative, that contribute to this condition. Thank you."

Place a soft fist below your jaw (as if you were posing for a cheesy portrait). Open your mouth slightly depressing your jaw into your fist. Hold and silently count to 7.

Then, gently close your mouth and relax your jaw. Count to three. Repeat these steps at least 3 times, or until your jaw feels more relaxed. Don't use any force when doing this exercise, all movements should be gentle.

Now, visualise your hands are transmitting orange lights. Put them a few inches from your jaw and transfer the orange light into your jaw doing clockwise movements.

Say: "Intuitive Healing Power please instil the feelings of confidence, self-expression and honesty into my jaw. Allow me to speak about my feelings freely and openly. Thank you."

Massage your jaw. Start with gentle tapping over the length of your jaw, and then do a circular massage using three fingers. Continue for 3-5 minutes or until the skin is tingling.

Say: "Intuitive Healing Power please heal and rejuvenate my jaw to its maximum health and vitality. Thank you."

When going to bed ask for a healing dream. Say: "Can I have a dream to help me heal my jaw and make me feel loving, secure and confident."

Emotional release: To complete the process of healing work on releasing stress, anger, guilt, judgment and frustration.

Colour therapy: You should work with orange and green for cleansing. Use pink to instil love.

Joints:

The joints represent flexibility and resilience to changes in life. Joint problems mean you become inflexible, stuck, pessimistic, critical, self-righteous and overwhelmed with hurts and responsibilities. You may be disconnected from the feelings of abundance and believe in lack: lack of money, lack of love, joy, opportunities and happiness, you are blocking and sabotaging yourself and putting the needs of others before your own.

Healing Technique:

Close your eyes and tune into the joints that are causing you pain. Ask yourself, "Where in my life do I block happiness and abundance? What is stopping me from moving forward towards my dreams?"

Listen to the answer. Don't judge, just acknowledge what you receive.

Breathe through your painful joints. Synchronise your breathing with the pain, do not resist it, the more you are able to relax through your pain the easier it gets.

Say: "Intuitive Healing Power please release all limitations, blockages, criticism and anger from my joints. Please remove all points of view that contribute to this condition. Thank you. "

Visualise your joints from the inside. Imagine a purple light entering your joints and starting to repair them. Feel the vibrations of this process.

Say: "Intuitive Healing Power please instil flexibility, lightness and strength into my joints. Allow me to move with ease and grace. Thank you."

Keep breathing through your painful joints and visualise your breath is cleaning and repairing them. Continue this for 15-20 minutes or until you feel lighter.

Say: "Intuitive Healing Power please heal and rejuvenate my joints to their maximum health and wellness. Thank you."

When you're going to bed ask for a healing dream. Say: "I need to experience a dream that helps me heal my joints and makes me experience ease, grace and love. Thank you."

Emotional release: Complete the process of healing by working on releasing stress, anger, guilt, judgment and criticism.

Colour therapy: Use purple, orange and green for cleaning and repairing. Use pink for love, gold for abundance.

Kidneys:

The kidneys represent your capacity to eliminate waste from the body. When you keep inside outdated beliefs and old hurts, they solidify, turn into stones and block your kidneys. If you're stuck in the past, holding on to resentment, guilt, criticism, disappointment and shame, your kidneys shut down. Long standing sadness, anger, giving up on your dreams can also contribute to serious kidney problems.

Healing Technique:

Relax. Visualise your kidneys. Tune into them. Breathe through your kidneys. Sense the subtle energy. Ask your kidneys: "What message are you trying to send me?" Listen to the answer....

Rub your hands together for 30 seconds to energise them. Place your hands 5-6 inches from your kidneys. Start a downward sweeping movement like you're trying to clean the area. Throw the toxic energy into the fire, a candle or an imaginary fire. Repeat the word 'Clear' a few times to strengthen the intention.

Say: "Intuitive Healing Power, please remove all sadness, anger, resentment and hurts from my kidneys as well as all points of view that contribute to this problem. Thank you."

Shake your hands like you are shaking off all the negative energy from them. Visualise your hands are transmitting a green light.

Place your hands over your kidneys and do clockwise movements. Visualise a green light is penetrating your kidneys, energising and repairing them.

Say: "Intuitive Healing Power, please instil strength, courage, happiness and joy into my body. Allow me to follow my intuitive guidance and make me feel confident and courageous. Thank you."

Put your hands firmly on your kidneys. Visualise them as healthy and vital. Breathe through your kidney.

Say: "Intuitive Healing Power, please heal and rejuvenate my kidneys to their maximum health and vitality. Thank you."

When you go to bed ask for a healing dream. Say: "Can I have a dream that helps me heal my kidneys and makes me feel light, spirited and empowered. Thank you." Write it down and put the request under your pillow. Go to sleep. Record your dreams first thing in the morning.

Emotional release: To complete the process of healing you must work on releasing emotions of sadness, fear, frustrations and guilt. Forgiveness is necessary to heal the kidneys.

Colour therapy: You should work with colours that promote cleansing, orange and green are good. Use pink to instil love.

Knees:

The knees symbolise your ability to be flexible while moving forward towards your dream. If you have problems here it means that you have become inflexible, stuck in the past with old issues, having regrets about unfulfilled dreams and think that life is unfair. Not trusting people, blaming and criticising.

Right Knee:

Issues with male side of family. Difficulty with making choices about career. Fear of failure. Pushing and forcing rather than allowing things to unfold.

Left Knee:

Issues with female side of family. Holding on to sadness, loss and grief from the past. Feeling like a victim. Not loving yourself. Complaining and blaming others.

Healing Technique:

Tune into your knee. Feel the sensations inside the joint. Breathe through the pain and discomfort. Describe your pain, is it sharp? What colour, temperature and texture? Breathe deeply and slowly. Synchronise with your pain. Every time you exhale visualise the reason for the pain is being expelled from your knee. Then visualise its gone.

Say: "Intuitive Healing Power, please dissolve all pain, anger, stiffness, rigidity, weakness, judgement and criticism from my knee. Please release all charge and all points of view that contributed to this problem. Thank you."

Rub your hands together for 30 seconds to energise them. Put your hands above your knee and start doing an anticlockwise movement like you are cleaning the air above the joint. Remove the negative energy and throw it into a fire, a candle or an imaginary fire. Repeat the word 'Clear' a few times to strengthen the intention and to clean the sore spot.

Visualise your hands are transmitting a green light. Transfer the green light into your knee by doing a clockwise movement with your hand.

Say: "Intuitive Healing Power, please instil strength, flexibility and confidence into my knee and let me move in the right direction with ease and grace. Thank you."

Massage your knee and continue bathing it with green light.

Say: "Intuitive Healing Power, please heal, restore and revitalise my knee to its ultimate health and vitality. Thank you."

Ask for a healing dream before going to bed. Say: "I need a dream to help me heal my knee and make me become flexible, light and confident. Thank you." Write the request on a paper and put it under the pillow. Record your dream first thing in the morning.

Emotional release: To complete the process of healing you must work on releasing emotions of anger, frustration control, criticism and stubbornness.

Colour therapy: You should work with green and orange for cleaning. Work with pink for love and acceptance.

Large Intestines:

The large intestines digest and absorb nutrients. If you experience problems here you have difficulty digesting life and coping with relationships. You feel insecure and unprotected when it comes to the energy of other people. You are frustrated, self-centred and sensitive, wanting to hide or run away from everybody in order to avoid problems rather than deal with them.

Healing Technique:

Relax. Tune into your large intestines, visualise them and breathe through them. Sense the subtle energy. Notice if the area feels blocked, depleted or empty? Ask yourself, "What am I hiding from? Whose negative energy do I absorb and keep in my body?" Listen to the answer....

Rub your hands together for 30 seconds to energise them. Place your hands 5-6 inches from your large intestines. Start a downward sweeping movement like you're cleaning something. Visualise removing all negative energy that you have absorbed from other people. Repeat the word 'Clear' a few times to enhance the intention.

Say: "Intuitive Healing Power, please remove all pain, toxicity, blockages and negativity from my intestines. Thank you."

Imagine a green light entering your abdomen and healing and purifying your large intestines.

Say: "Intuitive Healing Power, please instil strength, courage, happiness and joy into my intestines. Allow me to experience ease and grace. Thank you."

Put your hands firmly on your belly. Visualise your intestines as healthy and vital. Breathe through your intestines and sense the energy. Continue for 20 minutes.

Say: "Intuitive Healing Power, please heal and rejuvenate my intestines to their maximum health and wellness. Thank you."

Every day use an energy protection technique such as a shielding technique: Visualise a golden shield around your body which protects your energy field and repels negativity. Also use water to remove the negative energy from your body. Wash your face and your hands and visualise washing away the negativity. Repeat the word 'Clear' a few times to strengthen the intention.

Before going to bed say: "Intuitive Healing Power, please send me a dream to experience love, peace and joy. This dream will help me heal my intestines. Thank you." Write the request down on a piece of paper. Put it under your pillow. Go to sleep and don't allow any other thoughts to enter your mind. Record your dreams first thing in the morning.

Emotional release: To complete the process of healing you must work on releasing emotions of stress, fear, frustrations and judgment.

Colour therapy: You should work with colours that promote cleansing – orange and green. Also work with yellow for healthy self-esteem and with pink for unconditional love.

Legs:

The legs symbolise your ability to move forward towards your dreams. Leg problems show that your life is stressful and full of demands, that you are holding onto unresolved conflicts from the past and buying into self-doubt and insecurity. You may have problems with belonging and may be thinking, "Where do I belong? Whom do I belong with?"

Right Leg:

You are experiencing problems with taking actions, and are in conflict with masculine energy. Sabotaging yourself, doubts about the direction you are going and feeling dominated by a man in your life.

Left Leg:

You are being a people pleaser. Fear of moving forward and taking responsibility. Holding onto past conflicts, feeling like a victim; difficulty expressing your female energy or being in conflict with a woman in your family.

Healing Technique:

To heal you should love your legs. Thank them for carrying you around. Create a daily routine to show them your love. Massage your legs daily with oil and a moisturising cream. While massaging say: "Thank you for carrying me around. Thank you for letting me walk, dance, jog, jump, and move around. I love you, I love you, I love you."

Become aware of what you are carrying on your legs. Ask yourself, "What baggage do I carry? Who and what are holding me back? In what way do I sabotage myself?"

Become aware of the problems and then release them.

Say: "Intuitive Healing Power please release all burdens, insecurity, doubt, conflict and victimhood from my legs. Thank you."

Repeat the word 'Clear' a few times to strengthen the intention.

Visualise your leg as vital and healthy. Breathe throw your legs and sense a tingling sensation in your legs. Scan your legs with your attention. Start scanning from your feet and move up to your thighs, notice if there are any energy changes, density, dullness, or other sensations in your legs.

Stand up straight. Feel the ground with your feet. Visualise a red light entering your legs from the ground and moving up your both legs. Red is the colour of strength, power and vigour. Feel that your legs are becoming stronger and healthier.

Say: "Intuitive Healing Power please instil the feelings of confidence, courage, and self-empowerment into my legs. Thank you."

Breathe through your legs for 5-7 min. Sense the subtle energy inside your legs. Say: "Intuitive Healing Power, please heal and rejuvenate my legs to their maximum health and mobility. Thank you."

Before going to bed ask for a healing dream. Say: "I want a dream that will empower me to move forward towards my dreams. Thank you." Focus on your legs while trying to fall asleep.

Emotional release: To complete the process of healing you must release the emotions of anger, feelings of being overwhelmed, fear, frustrations and judgment.

Colour therapy: You should work with red, pink, orange and blue.

Liver:

The liver stores your negativity, anger and rage. Liver problems imply that you are sabotaging your own progress, experiencing inner conflict and feeling like a victim. You may be blaming others for your failures and using a 'poor me' attitude, thinking, "I'm right but nobody will listen." You may also have difficulty making decisions, inability to relax and not trusting life.

Healing Technique:

Close your eyes and tune into your liver. Visualise it. Talk to your liver. Ask: "What emotional baggage do I hold inside my liver?" Listen to the answers...

Just acknowledging these facts will release some blocked energy from your body and allow you to heal faster.

Rub your hands together for 30 seconds to sensitise them. Put your hand 5-6 inches from your liver. Start a downward sweeping motion. Visualise you are sweeping away negative energy from this area. Say: "Intuitive Healing Power, please release all pain, negativity, toxicity and struggle from my liver. Please remove all negative charge and all points of view that contribute to this problem. Thank you."

Repeat the word 'Clear' a few times to make your intentions stronger. Continue the downward sweeping for 3-4 minutes or until you feel lighter.

Continue the cleaning and purification with an anticlockwise movement over your liver for another 3-4 minutes. Then visualise your hands are transmitting a green light, put the green energy into the body by using a clockwise movement over your liver. Say "Intuitive Healing Power, please instil strength, confidence, relaxation and power into my system. Allow me to trust life and follow my intuition. Thank you."

Breathe through your liver for a few minutes and smile. Transfer the energy of your smile into your liver and visualise that your liver is smiling.

Say: "Intuitive Healing Power, please heal and rejuvenate my liver with happiness, joy and love. Thank you."

Before going to bed ask for a healing dream. Say: "I need to experience a dream which will assist me in healing my liver and to bring me feelings of joy, peace and love. Thank you." Write this request on a piece of paper and put it under your pillow. Record your dream in the morning.

Emotional release: To complete the process of healing you must release stress, anger, frustration, jealousy, control and guilt. Go through forgiveness.

Colour therapy: You should work with green for cleansing. Use yellow for self-esteem and happiness.

Lungs:

The lungs allow you to breathe. They also store energy which you breathe in. Lung problems mean that you are feeling sad, depressed, weepy and anguished. You suffer from low self-worth and feel smothered or overprotected. You hold on to grief and have difficulty expressing yourself and standing up for yourself. You are putting people's needs first, your own needs second. You are too much depended on others, needing their constant approval to do things.

Healing Technique:

The lungs represent your capacity to breathe and feel free, too much unexpressed emotions make your lungs congested. You need to learn a daily routine to clean your energy and remove toxicity from your lungs.

Sit comfortably. Tune into your lungs and feel the subtle energy inside. Breathe deeply and slowly. Visualise your lungs. Ask: "What destructive emotions do I keep in my chest? Whose needs do I put before my own needs? Who makes me feel smothered?" Acknowledge these answers, when exhaling visualise expelling negativity from your lungs.

Rub your hands together for 30 seconds to energise them. Place your hands over your lungs without touching and feel the energy they emit. Start a downward sweeping motion. Visualise you are sweeping away all pain, congestion, negativity and toxins. Remove and throw the negative energy in the fire, a candle or an imaginary fire. Repeat the word 'Clear' a few times to strengthen the intention. Continue sweeping for 5-10 minutes or until you feel lighter.

Say: "Intuitive Healing Power, please remove all sadness, depression, dependence and suppression from my lungs." Visualise a dark cloud leaving your chest.

Visualise your hands are transmitting an orange light. Place your hands over your lungs and transmit the orange light into your lungs by doing a clockwise movement. Bathe your lungs with orange. Orange is a great colour for rapid cleaning of the airways, it also stimulates vitality and boosts the immune system in the lungs.

Say: "Intuitive Healing Power, please instil happiness, vigour and confidence into my lungs. Allow me to breathe easily, deeply and freely. Thank you."

Repeat the process above by visualising an emerald light. Emerald energy will induce healing, growth of healthy tissue and calms your breathing.

Say: "Intuitive Healing Power, please heal, rejuvenate and restore my lungs to their maximum strength and vitality. Thank you."

Before going to sleep ask for a healing dream. Say: "I need to experience a dream that will help me feel loved, loving, supported and protected. This love can heal my lungs and allow me to breathe easily and freely. Thank you." Write it on a piece of paper and put this paper under your pillow.

Emotional release: To complete the process of healing you must work on releasing emotions of anger, sadness, frustration and low self-esteem.

Colour therapy: You should work with orange and green for cleaning the bad energy.

Mouth:

The mouth represents 'speaking your truth'. Mouth problems mean you are not speaking your truth, having a closed mind, and being stuck in your old way of doing things. You may be saying things you don't like, feeling angry with yourself and others, not expressing yourself and trying to please others and clinging to people.

Healing Technique:

Tune into your mouth. Feel the subtle energy. Become aware of the condition of your tongue, gums, teeth and lips. What taste is in your mouth? How fresh is your breath? Can you chew food properly? Can you swallow freely? Do you rush when you eat? Do you rush when you talk? Are your teeth good? Are your gums healthy?

Start cleaning your mouth daily. Take a table spoon of baking soda and dissolve it in a glass of warm water, rinse your mouth daily with this solution. When you are rinsing, visualise purifying your mouth with a white colour.

Say: "Intuitive Healing Power, please remove bad attitudes, close-mindedness, judgment and criticism from my mouth. Please release all points of view that contribute to this condition. Thank you."

When you are spitting out the solution, visualise you are spitting out problems from your mouth.

Repeat the word 'Clear' a few times to enhance the intention.

After rinsing, visualise an orange light entering your mouth. Orange rays clean, rejuvenate and instil more confidence in your mouth.

Say: "Intuitive Healing Power, please instil confidence, self-esteem, pride, happiness and joy into my mouth. Thank you."

Breathe through your mouth. Visualise your mouth becoming fresher with every breath.

Say: "Intuitive Healing Power, please heal and restore my mouth to its maximum health. Thank you."

Ask for a healing dream. Say: "I want a dream to help me speak my truth, express my needs clearly and become more confident and creative. Thank you."

Emotional release: To complete the process of healing your mouth you must release worry, criticism, frustration and low self-esteem.

Colour therapy: You should work with green and white for cleansing. Work with orange for rejuvenation, self-esteem and confidence. Use pink for love and use gold for abundance.

Muscles:

Your muscles symbolise your power and ability to act, move and overcome difficulties. Muscle problems mean you have a lot of strain due to work and many responsibilities. You may act like or are a workaholic. You may be resistant to accept new experiences and not able to move forward. You are worrying about self-image and stuck in continuous stress.

Healing Technique:

Sit on a chair or crossed leg on the floor. Open your hands. Tune into your muscles. Breathe through the tension and pain. Feel the energy.

To heal your muscles you must keep them relaxed. To evoke relaxation response you must know the difference between tension and relaxation in your muscles. Many people become accustomed to their tension and forget what relaxation feels like.

Now we will try to tense and relax each muscle group in your body.

Start from your feet. Lift up your toes and tense all the muscles in your feet. Keep the tension for a few seconds and release. Feel the difference between tension and relaxation.

Focus on your calf muscles and tense them as much as you can. Hold this tension for a few seconds and release. Feel the difference between tension and relaxation.

Focus on your upper legs, tense them and then release the tension. Feel the difference between tension and relaxation.

Tense your buttocks, hold the tension for a few seconds and release. Feel the difference.

Tense and relax your abdomen. Feel the difference.

Tense and relax your chest. Feel the difference.

Tense and relax your shoulders and arms. Feel the difference.

Tense and relax your hands. Feel the difference.

Tense and relax your neck muscles. Feel the difference.

Tense and relax your mouth, cheeks, and forehead. Feel the difference.

Practice this tension and relaxation technique until you are completely comfortable with it. Do it every day.

Say: "Intuitive Healing Power, please remove all tension, stress and feelings of being overwhelmed from my muscles. Thank you. "

Keep breathing and feel all your muscles relax.

Say: "Intuitive Healing Power please heal and rejuvenate my muscles. Thank you. "

When going to bed, order a healing dream. Say: "I need to experience a dream to help me heal my muscles and restore my confidence, self-love and self-acceptance. Thank you." Write these words on a piece of paper and put this under your pillow. Go to sleep.

Emotional release: To complete the process of healing you must work on releasing anger, stress, sadness, being overwhelmed and frustrated. Forgive yourself and others.

Colour therapy: You should work with green and orange for cleaning the negativity. Use blue for relieving stress.

Nails:

The nails protect the tips of your fingers and toes. Nails show how well you protect your sensitivity. If you have problems, you are probably frustrated, annoyed, stressed and irritable. You may have been overwhelmed with your relationship problems and feel that you're wasting time on something. You are suppressing your emotions and blaming other people for how you feel.

Healing Technique:

Relax and tune into your nails. Ask yourself, "Who and what do I hide under my nails? What irritable feelings do I hold onto?" Listen to the answer.

Admitting what you feel irritable will release blocked energy. Give this emotion a name: anger, frustration, irritation or fear.

When you name it, pull the emotion from the affected finger using the other hand. Say: "I am removing anger...I am removing fear... I am removing irritation etc." Throw the negative emotions into the fire. Light a candle or visualise a fire.

Rub your hands together for 30 seconds. Place your hands slightly apart and feel the energy between them. Imagine this energy is pure white. Bathe your nails with pure white energy. Clean and energise them.

Say: "Intuitive Healing Power, please clean and purify my nails. Thank you."

Do the same process with a green colour.

Say: "Intuitive Healing Power, please heal and rejuvenate my nails. Thank you."

Ask for a healing dream. Say: "I want to experience a dream that helps me become confident, safe and secure. Thank you."

Emotional release: To complete the process of healing you must work on releasing stress, worry, and frustration. Forgive yourself and others.

Colour therapy: You should work with white, green and orange.

Neck:

The neck represents flexibility. Neck problems mean you are prone to be inflexible and stubborn, disconnected from your heart, having relationship problems and holding on to past hurts. You are refusing to accept the point of view of others, and engage in too much thinking.

Healing Technique:

Start the healing process from assessing your attitudes and lifestyle. Ask yourself, "Have I called something or someone a pain in the neck? Do I feel strangled with my commitments? Do I speak from my heart? Do I lie to myself?"

Now tune into your neck and sense the energy. Ask: "If my neck had a memory what would it be? If my neck had an emotion what would it would be? If my neck had a picture of itself what would it be? Would it be hard like a tree trunk, or soft and gentle, flexible like rubber?"

Listen to the answer...Acknowledging these truths will release blocked energy from your neck.

Breathe deeply and slowly through your neck, try to imagine you can breathe through your neck. Relax. Tilt your head back, and with your both hands, squeeze the flesh at the base of your neck on either side of your spine. Then, slowly roll your head forward, still squeezing your skin. Hold the stretch for 10 seconds, and then return your head to an upright position. Repeat this movement 5 times.

Every time you're releasing the stretch visualise releasing the stubbornness, inflexibility and one-sidedness.

Say: "Intuitive Healing Power, please release all fear, stress and tightness from my neck. Thank you." Repeat the word 'Clear' a few times to enhance the intention.

Visualise your hands are transmitting a green light. Stroke your neck up and down with your hands, bathing your neck with green light.

Say: "Intuitive Healing Power, please instil flexibility, self-expression, patience and truth into my body. Allow me to let go of the past and let me move forward towards the future. Thank you."

Then use your fingers on both hands make a deep circular motion pressing around the neck area.

Say: "Intuitive Healing Power, please heal and rejuvenate my neck back to its maximum health and wellness."

Before going to bed ask for a healing dream. Say: "I want to experience a dream that helps me become light, flexible and joyful. Thank you."

Emotional release: To complete the process of healing you must work on releasing stress, worry, feeling stuck and frustration.

Colour therapy: Use green for cleansing and blue for calming and relaxation.

Nervous system:

The nervous system represents your connections between the internal and the external worlds. If this connection is unbalanced you experience stress, feeling under threat and your nervous system works in a continuous 'fight and flight' mode. You are prone to hold onto insecurity, shame and guilt, trying to act like a workaholic but only compromising yourself as a result. You may be using food, drugs or alcohol to compensate for your stress. Or you're looking for instant pleasures and fixes which make you even more unbalanced and weak.

Healing Technique:

Sit and relax. Breathe deeply and focus on the centre of your body. Open your palms so that they are facing upwards. This position shows that you are ready to receive intuitive energy.

Slowly count from 10 to 1.

Visualise a blue light entering your body through the top of your head. It streams down your spine branching out to every part of your anatomy until your whole body is bathed with blue. Feel the relaxation, calmness and peace that come with it.

Imagine that this blue light is cleaning and purifying your body. Feel that with every exhale you release stress and tension from your system.

Say: "Intuitive Healing Power, please release all stress, burdens, impatience, attack, threat and insecurity from my nervous system. Let me remove all charge and all points of view that contribute to this problem. Thank you."

Repeat the word 'Clear' a few times to enhance the intention.

Visualise yourself swimming in a blue ocean or floating in a blue river. You can soak your body in a blue bath and light blue candles. Turn on music that is calming.

Say: "Intuitive Healing Power, please instil calmness, relaxation, balance, peace and joy into my nervous system. Thank you."

Scan your body with your mind's eye bit by bit starting from your toes up to your trunk, chest, neck and head. Relax every part of your body one by one.

Say: "I am releasing tension from my toes... I am releasing tension from my legs... I am releasing tension from my buttocks.... I am releasing tension from my abdomen... I am releasing tension from my chest... I am releasing tension from my neck... I am releasing tension from my head..."

Say: "Intuitive Healing Power, please heal and rejuvenate my nervous system. Thank you."

Before going to bed ask for a healing dream. Say: "I need to experience a dream that brings peace and relaxation into my body and rejuvenates my nervous system entirely. Thank you."

Emotional release: To complete the process of healing you must work on releasing stress, attack, worry, frustration and shame.

Colour therapy: You should work with blue and green for cleaning and calming. Work with gold for energising. Work with white for purification.

Nose:

The nose helps you to smell. Smell is one of the most powerful senses that can stimulate memories and affect your whole wellbeing. Nose problems indicate that you are sensitive and overwhelmed with emotions, looking for attention and seeking somebody to love you. You are prone to become judgmental, critical, sticking your nose into somebody else's affairs and not looking after your own.

Healing Technique:

Tune into your nose. What can your nose tell you? What emotions does it keep? What memories does it have? Listen to the answers…

The nose is an intuitive tool. It brings valuable information about people and places. You must learn to trust your nose.

Rub your hands together for 30 seconds. Visualise your hands transmitting an indigo light. Put your hands on your nose and bathe your nose and sinuses with the indigo colour.

Say: "Intuitive Healing Power, please release all blockages, criticism, unworthiness and judgement from my nose. Please remove all points of view and all charge, negative and positive that contribute to this problem. Thank you."

Repeat the word 'Clear' a few times to enhance the intention.

With your middle finger press a point which is located just above the bridge of your nose, in between your eyebrows. Keep pressure for 1-2 minutes. Visualise an indigo ray coming from the tip of your middle finger into your nose. Repeat the words: "Clear, clear, clear."

With both middle fingers, press the points that are located on the sides of your nostrils. Keep pressure for 1-2 minutes. Visualise indigo rays coming from the tips of both your fingers. Repeat the words: "Clear, clear, clear."

With both index fingers, press the points that are located at the very top of your nose, just at the point where your nose connects to the ridge of your eyebrows. Keep pressure for 1-2 minutes. Visualise indigo rays coming out of the tips of both fingers. Repeat the words: "Clear, clear, clear."

With your index finger, press the point that is located just under your nose, in a little groove that you can feel on your upper lip. To activate this point press in and upwards against the base of the nose. Keep pressure for 1-2 minutes. Visualise indigo rays coming from the tips of your fingers. Repeat the words: "Clear, clear, clear."

Visualise your nose becoming clearer, healthier and lighter.

Before going to bed ask for a healing dream. Say: "I need to experience a dream that will help me connect to my intuition and Divine wisdom."

Emotional release: To complete the process of healing your nose work on releasing stress, judgment, criticism, hurt and worry.

Colour therapy: You should work with blue for calming and decongestion, with green for clearing, with white for purification, with purple and indigo for clarity and stabilisation.

Oesophagus:

The oesophagus helps you to swallow food. If you have problems here, you have difficulty tolerating (or swallowing) something or someone in your life. You are holding onto grief and hurt, thinking that you're unimportant or second best, lying to yourself and hiding behind a mask.

The Secret Energy of Your Body | 117

Healing Technique:

Tune into your oesophagus. Visualise it. Breathe through it. If your oesophagus could talk what would it say? What memories does it hold? Who and what is it you can't swallow?

Become aware of all emotions that contribute to this problem.

Rub your hands together for 30 seconds. Place your hands over your oesophagus without touching the body and start a downward sweeping movement. Visualise you are sweeping away all blockages and negativity.

Say: "Intuitive Healing Power, please release unworthiness, low self-esteem, criticism, negativity and judgment from my oesophagus. Please remove all points of view that contribute to this problem. Thank you."

Repeat the word 'Clear' to enhance the intention.

Visualise an orange light moving in to your oesophagus and energising it. Say: "Intuitive Healing Power, please install confidence, self-worth, love, happiness and joy into my system. Thank you."

Breathe deeply through your oesophagus. Sense the subtle energy inside it. Say: "Intuitive Healing Power, please heal and rejuvenate my oesophagus. Thank you."

Visualise your oesophagus becoming clearer, healthier and lighter.

Before going to sleep ask for a healing dream. Say: "I need to experience a dream to make me feel safe, secure, supported and protected. These feelings will heal me and my oesophagus. Thank you."

Emotional release: To complete the process of healing, work on releasing sadness, low self-esteem, judgment, hurt and worry.

Colour therapy: You should work with orange and green for cleaning, blue for calming and relaxing.

Ovaries:

The ovaries represent your creativity and femininity. Ovary problems show that you are rejecting your femininity and creativity and not enjoying your womanhood. You hold onto your wounds, especially associated with men and believe you are aging too fast. You worry about things and don't trust your intuition. You tend to force things rather than letting them unfold naturally.

Healing Technique:

To heal your ovaries you need to enjoy being a woman. In what way do you undermine your femininity? Are you the one who looks after everybody and forgets to meet her own needs? Do you say to yourself that you can't afford something but if this was for your husband, child or other you would buy it without hesitation?

You must become aware of your personal needs and desires and act lovingly towards yourself. Ask yourself, "What things do I love to have? What things do I love to do? What are my dreams? What do I deserve in my life?"

If you have difficulty answering these questions, than complete these sentences which will help you to define your dreams and desires:

1. My favourite childhood toy was .....
2. My favourite childhood game was...
3. My five favourite movies are .....
4. My five favourite activities when I was a youth were....
5. My five favourite songs are.....
6. My five favourite books are....
7. My favourite way to dress is....

Look for a common theme that emerges when answering these questions. The theme is a clue to what you should be doing to enjoy your life. This will help you to recover your sense of power, the power you need to heal your illness. Allow yourself to enjoy your feminine power and embrace your sensuality. Realise that being feminine and sensual is beautiful and powerful.

Say: "Intuitive Healing Power, please release all guilt, stress, resistance and all points of view that stop me from expressing my femininity. Please release unworthiness, weakness and disempowerment from my ovaries. Thank you."

Repeat the word 'Clear' a few times to enhance the intention.

Rub your hands together for 30 seconds. Place your hands over your ovaries without touching the body. Start downward sweeping motions. Visualise you're cleaning your ovaries.

Say: "Intuitive Healing Power, please purify my ovaries from negativity and install confidence, love, honour and good values into my ovaries. Let me love and appreciate myself. Thank you."

Imagine your hands are transmitting orange lights. Start a clockwise movement with your hands over your ovaries. Feel that the orange energy is penetrating your ovaries.

Say: "Intuitive Healing Power, please heal, restore and rejuvenate my ovaries. Thank you."

Ask for a healing dream. Say: "Can I experience a dream which helps me become feminine and joyful. Thank you."

Emotional release: To complete the process of healing you must work on releasing stress, anger, hurt, resentment and sadness. Forgive yourself and others.

Colour therapy: You should work with orange, gold, yellow and green.

Pancreas:

The pancreas controls the production of chemicals to break down food. The organ starts to malfunction when you stop enjoying your life, taking too much responsibility onto yourself, feeling trapped in a situation, smothered or under-nurtured. You may experience continuous hopelessness, over-concern and lack of control. You hold on to bitterness, confusion, unfairness and low self-esteem. You believe that life has lost its sweetness and you start looking for quick fixes. You can be easily swayed in one situation but stubborn and unmovable in another.

Healing Technique:

Tune into your pancreas. Visualise it and sense the energy inside. Ask yourself, "In what way have I stopped enjoying my life? What bitterness do I hold inside?" Just acknowledging these truths will release some blocked energy from your body.

Breathe through your pancreas for 5-6 minutes. Keep sensing the subtle energy.

Put your hands over your solar plexus; the organ which energetically controls your pancreas. Let the tips of your fingers join together, but pointing away from you. Cross the thumbs. It is important to straighten the fingers. Chant the sound 'RAM' and sense the vibrations of this sound in your pancreas. Hold this pose for 5 minutes.

Rub your hands together for 30 seconds. Place them over your pancreas and start a downward sweeping motion. Visualise you're cleaning and purifying the organ.

Say: "Intuitive Healing Power, please remove all bitterness, confusion, helplessness and hopelessness from my pancreas and the related organs. Thank you."

Visualise your hands are transmitting a yellow ray. Start a clockwise movement with your hands over your pancreas and solar plexus.

Say: "Intuitive Healing Power, please instil confidence, kindness, love and honour into my pancreas and related organs. Let me love and appreciate myself. Thank you."

Repeat the word 'Clear' a few times to enhance the intention. Feel the vibrations of the yellow rays inside your pancreas.

Say: "Intuitive Healing Power, please heal and rejuvenate my pancreas. Thank you."

Before going to bed ask for a healing dream. Say: "I need a dream which can heal my pancreas and bring me the feelings of sweetness, loveliness and joy. Thank you."

Emotional release: To complete the process of healing you must work on releasing frustrations, control, stress, anger, guilt, resentment and rejection. Forgive yourself and others.

Colour therapy: Work with orange and yellow for cleaning and strengthening. Work with pink for love and sweetness.

Penis:

The penis represents masculine power. If you have problems there you are feeling vulnerable, sensitive, unlovable, depressed, having low self-esteem and holding on to criticism and judgment. You hold on to fears especially related to intimacy and love. You carry hurts from a person who was close, you don't trust others and feel victimised and rejected, stuck in the past.

Healing Technique:

To heal you must acknowledge and release all suppressed emotions that contribute to this condition. Ask yourself, "Where do these feelings of hurt and resentment come from? Who are these people who hurt me? Am I willing to forgive them?"

Name these people. Imagine that this person sits in front of you. Visualise the energetic connection between you and the person as an energy cord that runs from your abdomen to his/her abdomen. Visualise this cord.

Now, lift your hand up and chop this cord. Do the same with another hand. Repeat 3 times with each hand. Visualise the cord is cut and has disappeared.

Say: "Intuitive Healing Power, please cut all negative attachments between me and ....(say the person's name). I am letting this person go and forgiving him/her all things he/she has ever done to me. Thank you."

Rub your hands together for 30 seconds. Place your hands over the lower abdominal area and start a sweeping motion. Visualise that you are sweeping all negative energy and blockages away.

Say: "Intuitive Healing Power, please release all feelings of rejection, anger, hurt and victimisation from my reproductive organs. Thank you."

Continue cleaning the same area with an anticlockwise movement of your hand.

Say: "Intuitive Healing Power, please help me forgive this person (say name). Thank you."

Visualise that you are feeling lighter and lighter.

Say: "Intuitive Healing Power, please heal and rejuvenate my reproductive organs to their maximum health and vitality. Thank you."

Before going to bed ask for a healing dream. Say: "I need to experience a dream that helps me forgive and let go of my past. Thank you."

Emotional release: To complete the process of healing you must work on releasing fear, stress, anger, guilt, resentment and rejection. Forgive yourself and others.

Colour therapy: Work with orange and green for cleaning and strengthening. Work with red for sexual power. Work with pink for love. Work with turquoise for freedom and liberation.

Pineal Glands:

The pineal glands control the production of your hormones and regulate your sleep-awake pattern. It constitutes for a 'third eye' – the centre of your intuition. Problems with these glands mean that you are disconnected, isolated, confused and ignoring your intuition. You have a skeptical view of life and feel stuck, doubtful and insecure.

Healing Technique:

Tune into your pineal glands. Ask yourself, "In what way do I compromise myself? Who and what is stopping me from listening to my intuition?"

Visualise your pineal glands. See it as a luminous orb in the middle of your head. It emits light to your whole energy system. Breathe deeply and sense the energy inside your head.

Say: "Intuitive Healing Power, please release all confusion, separation, uncertainty, skepticism and doubt from my mind as well as all points of view that contribute to this condition. Thank you."

Repeat the word 'Clear' a few times to enhance the intention.

Imagine the luminous orb in the middle of your head transmitting indigo lights. Indigo helps to improve vision, intuition and clean mental dullness. Bathe your whole head with indigo.

Say: "Intuitive Healing Power, please connect me to my intuition, bring balance and harmony into my life. Thank you."

Breathe deeply and slowly. Exhale through your head. Visualise releasing all tension with each exhale.

Say: "Intuitive Healing Power, please heal and revive my pineal glands. Thank you."

Before going to bed say: "I need to experience a dream that helps me relax and connect to my intuition. Thank you."

Emotional release: To complete the process of healing you must work on releasing low self-esteem, fear, frustration and being overwhelmed.

Colour therapy: Work with indigo and purple to strengthen your intuition and bring mental clarity.

Pituitary Glands:

The pituitary glands control all other glands in your body and produce hormones related to growth, sexual development, metabolism and reproduction. If you have problems with your pituitary you experience sluggishness, dismay, confusion and have many fears. You are holding onto past hurts and have problems with forgiving yourself and others.

Healing Technique:

Tune into your pituitary glands. Imagine your pituitary is a golden pea sitting on a purple throne. Ask yourself, "How do I compromise this 'princess'? What kind of thoughts and behaviours could damage it? Who and what can't I forgive and let go of?" Listen to the answers...

Rub your hands together for 30 seconds. Place them slightly apart and visualise indigo lights between your palms. Place your hands over the sides of your head and transfer this indigo light to your pituitary. Indigo is the colour of clarity and mental calmness.

Say: "Intuitive Healing Power, please release all confusion, tiredness, fear and threat my pituitary glands. Thank you."

Repeat the word 'Clear' a few times to strengthen the intention.

Place your middle finger between your eyebrows. Visualise a straight line between your finger and your pituitary gland. Say: "Intuitive Healing Power, please instil clarity, strengths, power and brightness into my pituitary gland. Let me experience joy, stability and security in my life. Thank you."

With your middle and ring fingers massage the area between your eyebrows, then massage your temples. Then put your left hand on your forehead and your right hand on the back of your head and massage these areas simultaneously.

Say: "Intuitive Healing Power, please heal and rejuvenate my pituitary glands to their maximum health and wellness. Thank you."

Ask for a healing dream before going to bed. Say: "I want a dream that instils clarity and strength into my thoughts and helps me heal my pituitary glands. Thank you." Write it on a piece of paper and put it under your pillow. Record your dream first thing in the morning.

Emotional release: To complete the process of healing you must work on releasing fear, feelings of being stuck, low self-esteem, and depression.

Colour therapy: Work with indigo and purple to restore your mental clarity and intuitive connection.

Prostate Gland:

The prostate stands for masculine strength. Problems here imply that you are feeling ashamed, suppressed, inferior, not as good as others. You hold on to resentment, disappointment and betrayal. Feel insecure, unsafe, unsupported and unable to forgive.

Healing Technique:

Take a few deep breaths. Connect to the stillness inside you. Ask yourself, "Why do I feel like a failure? Who can't I forgive? What things do I hold onto that I must let go?"

Become aware of your feelings and allow yourself to express them. Visualise a person who has hurt you and say what you feel. Breathe deeply and slowly. Visualise that with every breath out you release the feelings associated with this person. Feel lighter and lighter.

Rub your hands together for 30 seconds. Place your hand over your prostate. Start a downward sweeping movement. Visualise sweeping all negativity, hurt and blockages away from this organ. Say: "Intuitive Healing Power, please remove all shame, guilt, fear and feelings of being stuck from my reproductive system. Please dissolve all preconceived ideas and all points of view that contribute to this problem. Thank you."

Visualise that your hands are transmitting an orange light. Start a clockwise movement over your prostate putting this energy in and say: "Intuitive Healing Power, please instil confidence, security, strength and power into my prostate. Thank you." Continue for 3-4 minutes.

Do the same process with a green light and say: "Intuitive Healing Power, please heal and restore my prostate gland and all relevant organs. Thank you."

Ask for a healing dream: "Can I please have a dream that makes me feel strong and masculine and helps me heal my reproductive organs. Thank you."

Emotional release: To complete the process of healing you must work on releasing shame, guilt, fear, feelings of being stuck, low self-esteem, and depression. Forgive yourself and others.

Colour therapy: Work with green, orange and yellow.

Rib cage:

The rib cage protects your lungs and symbolises protection of the breath of life. Problems imply that you feel unsafe, burdened by doubts and self-sabotage. You feel vulnerable, insecure and block new possibilities in life.

Healing Technique:

Take a few deep breaths and tune into your ribs. Become aware of all the structures inside. Breathe through the ribs. Whilst inhaling, focus on expanding your rib cage. Whilst exhaling, focus on releasing pain and negative energy.

Say: "Intuitive Healing Power, please release all pain, blockages, burdens and doubts from my ribs. Please dissolve all points of view that contribute to this condition.

Repeat the word 'Clear' a few times to enhance the intention.

Rub your hands together until they tingle. Put your hands over your ribs and start a downward sweeping movement. Continue for 2-3 minutes or until you feel lighter.

Then visualise that your palms are transmitting a green light. Transfer this green to your rib cage by doing a clockwise movement with your hands. Bathe your ribs with green light.

Say: "Intuitive Healing Power, please instil strength, confidence and the sense of safety into my rib cage. Allow me to feel secure and certain. Thank you."

Gently massage your ribs with a stroking and circular movement. Say: "Intuitive Healing Power, please heal and rejuvenate my rib cage and all related organs. Thank you."

Ask for a healing dream before going to bed. Say: "I want a dream that helps me heal my ribs and makes me feel safe, secure and protected. Thank you."

Emotional release: To complete the process of healing you must work on releasing low self-esteem, control and fear.

Colour therapy: Work with green for cleaning, work with orange for energising, yellow for cementing and strengthening your ribs.

Shins:

The shins represent quality of life. If you have problems here you feel disappointed with people in your life, betrayed, victimised and let down. You may be thinking of revenge and holding onto guilt, shame and inadequacy.

Healing Technique:

Tune into your shins. Breathe through your shins. Whilst exhaling focus on releasing pain and negative energy from them.

Say: "Intuitive Healing Power, please remove all anger, betrayal, guilt, self-punishment and victimhood from my shins. Help me to release all points of view that contribute to this problem. Thank you."

Rub your hands together until they tingle. Start a sweeping movement over your shins. Sweep away all pain, negativity and blockages from your shins.

Then visualise your palms are transmitting a green healing light. Put your hands over your shins and start a clockwise movement transferring green light into the bone. Bathe your shin with green light. Say: "Intuitive Healing Power, please instil strength, confidence and empowerment into my shins. Allow me to experience joy and power. Thank you."

Massage your shins with a stroking movement then with a circular movement.

Say: "Intuitive Healing Power, please heal and rejuvenate my shins to their maximum strength and vigour. Thank you."

Ask for a healing dream. Say: "I need a dream in which I experience the feelings of trust and empowerment. Thank you."

Emotional release: To complete the process of healing you must work on releasing low self-esteem, guilt, fear and judgment. Forgive yourself and others.

Colour therapy: Work with green for cleaning the energy. Work with pink to instil self-love.

Shoulders:

The shoulders symbolise 'carrying weight'. Problems here mean you are burdened with too much strain, stress and worry. You are the person who is 'carrying a world' on your shoulders and feel rejected, discouraged, easily hurt and frightened.

Healing Technique:

Sit, relax and focus on your breath. Ask yourself, "Who and what do I carry on my shoulders?" Become aware of your burdens and try to release them with every exhale.

Tune into your shoulders and visualise its structure. Describe your pain or discomfort. If the pain was an object, what would it be? Name the object (for example a ball, a splinter, a knife, a cloud etc). With your other hand remove this object from your shoulder.

Say: "Intuitive Healing Power, please remove all burdens, blockages, strain, insecurity, pain and weight from my shoulders. Please release all points of view that contribute to this condition. Thank you."

Place your left hand on your right shoulder and squeeze it. Hold the squeeze and slowly rotate your shoulder backwards. A grinding noise indicates that muscles are tense and should be freed up. Repeat with the right hand on the left shoulder.

Say: "Intuitive Healing Power, please instil ease, confidence and balance in to my shoulder. Thank you."

Pummel your right shoulder with your left hand to bring fresh blood to the area. Repeat on your left shoulder.

Tense your shoulders keep the tension for 5 seconds and relax. Repeat 10 times. Sense the energy flowing inside your shoulders.

Say: "Intuitive Healing Power, please heal, restore and rejuvenate my shoulders. Thank you."

Before going to bed ask for a healing dream. Say: "I need to experience a dream that helps me heal my shoulders and brings me the feeling of love, joy and support."

Emotional release: To complete the process of healing you must work on releasing worry, stress, guilt, hurt and feeling overwhelmed. Forgive yourself and others.

Colour therapy: Work with green for cleaning, use yellow for strengthening and pink for love.

Sinuses:

The sinuses produce mucous to moisturise inside the nose and protect the inner lining. Problems here show that you are feeling irritated, especially with someone close to you. You are not expressing yourself and hiding your true feelings about the situation. You have difficulty standing up for yourself and are torn between people and responsibilities. You are worn out, thinking too much, criticising, judging and not connecting to your intuition.

Healing Technique:

Tune into your sinuses. Become aware of the feelings that contribute to this condition. What feelings are you suppressing? Who are you giving your energy to and not getting anything in return? Acknowledge these truths and release the negativity when breathing and exhaling.

Rub your hands together until they tingle. Put your right hand over your sinuses without touching and start an anticlockwise movement. Feel that you're removing pain and density from your sinuses. Throw it in the fire, a candle or an imaginary fire.

Say: "Intuitive Healing Power, please remove all irritation, frustration, vulnerability and stress from my sinuses. Please release all charge, negative and positive and all points of view that contribute to this condition. Thank you." Repeat the word 'Clear' a few times to enhance the intention.

Massage the area around your nose with the tips of two fingers for 1 minute.

With your index fingers, press the spot located at the very top of the nose, where your nose connects to the ridge of your eyebrows. Keep pressure for 1-2 minutes. Visualise silver rays coming from the tips of both fingers and clear the sinuses. Repeat the word 'Clear' a few times.

Then press the spots that are located on the sides of your nostrils. Keep pressure for 1-2 minutes. Visualise silver rays coming from the tips of both your fingers into your sinuses and clear them. Repeat the word 'Clear' a few times.

Press the spot that is located just under your nose, in a little groove that you can feel on your upper lip. To activate this point press in and upwards against the base of the nose. Keep pressure for 1-2 minutes. Visualise silver rays and repeat the word 'Clear.'

Say: "Intuitive Healing Power, please instil safety, clarity and strength into my sinuses. Thank you."

Take a few deep breaths through your nose and feel the air going through your sinuses. Focus on your sinuses and visualise as if they are clear and healthy.

Say: "Intuitive Healing Power, please heal and restore my sinuses and all related organs to their maximum health and vitality. Thank you."

Before going to bed ask for a healing dream. Say: "I want a dream that helps me clear my sinuses and makes me feel light, easy and comfortable. Thank you."

Emotional release: To complete the process of healing you must work on releasing stress, worry, low self-esteem, fear and judgment. Forgive yourself and others.

Colour therapy: Work with blue, silver, indigo and violet.

Skeleton:

The skeleton represents the foundation and structure of the body. Problems imply that you are losing your structure and letting yourself down by criticising, judging, holding onto betrayal and guilt. You may also feel insecure and let down by people close to you.

Healing Technique:

Became aware of your negative emotions, what are the past relationships that are still causing you pain? Who are the people that you need to forgive? What are the 'skeletons' that you keep in your closet?

To heal, you must be completely honest with yourself. This honesty can be achieved through journaling, meditating and asking yourself the right questions. If you haven't started your intuitive healing journal yet begin it today.

Now, sit comfortably and relax. Take a few deep breaths. Open your hands and keep them on your lap. Let the tips of your thumb and index finger touch. Relax other fingers. Concentrate on the middle of your body and follow your breath. When inhaling feel that your body is expanding and rising. When exhaling feel that your body is descending. Continue for 3-5 minutes.

Chant the sound 'LAM' and feel the vibrations of this sound in your skeleton. Feel the energy of this vibration in the cells of your skeleton.

Say: "Intuitive Healing Power, please remove all negativity, betrayal, dishonesty, judgment and criticisms from my skeleton. Please release all charge and all points of view that contribute to this condition. Thank you."

Repeat the word 'Clear' a few times to enhance the intention. Visualise a green light entering your body from the top of your head, healing and energising your skeleton with the power of green.

Say: "Intuitive Healing Power, please instil the feelings of confidence, security, support and integrity into my skeleton. Thank you."

Bathe your whole body with green energy and feel lighter and lighter.

Say: "Intuitive Healing Power, please heal and regenerate my skeleton. Thank you."

Before going to bed ask, "I need a healing dream that makes me feel safe, secure, supported and protected. Thank you."

Emotional release: To complete the process of healing you must work on releasing low self-esteem, resentment, fear and judgment. Forgive yourself and others.

Colour therapy: Work with green for cleaning and energising, work with pink to instil love, work with purple and silver to get clarity and intuitive insight.

Skin:

The skin represents protection, boundaries, sensitivity and vulnerability. Skin problems show that you feel insecure, threatened, impatient, fearful and uncomfortable in your own skin. You are irritated with people and situations, feeling that you don't belong and are second best. You suppress your emotions and hide your truth.

Healing Technique:

Stand in front of a mirror, look into your own eyes, and ask yourself, "Who is getting under my skin? What truth am I hiding and not expressing? In what way do I compromise myself?" Listen to the answer.

Acknowledging this truth will help you release blocked energy immediately.

Say: "Intuitive Healing Power, please remove all anger, irritation, frustration, insecurity, inferiority from my skin. Please release all points of view that contribute to this condition. Thank you." Repeat the word 'Clear' to enhance the intention.

Imagine someone who loves you stands next to you. It can be a friend, your mother, father or other relative. Feel the energy of love from this person penetrates your whole body. Visualise pink light coming from this person and bathe your whole body with pink energy. Pink produces vibrations of love in your body. Feel it. Allow pink to penetrate all your skin cells and energise them.

Say: "Intuitive Healing Power, please make me feel comfortable, confident, secure and happy. Allow me to feel loved and loving. Thank you."

Sit comfortably, put your hands on your lap, let the tips of your index finger and thumb touch. Relax the other fingers. Concentrate on your heart and chant the sound 'YAM,' feel the vibration of this sound in your skin.

The frequency of this sound is similar to the frequency of a pink colour, and combined they generate vibrations of love.

Continue chanting and visualising pink for 5 minutes or until you feel lighter.

Say: "Intuitive Healing Power, please heal and rejuvenate my skin and all related organs to their maximum health and wellness. Allow me to feel loved and loving. Thank you."

Before going to bed ask for a healing dream. Say: "I want a dream that helps me experience unconditional love which will heal my skin and all related organs. Thank you."

Emotional release: To complete the process of healing you must work on releasing stress, worry, low self-esteem, being overwhelmed, hurt and resentment. Forgive yourself and others.

Colour therapy: You can use many colors to treat skin conditions. Use white and green for cleaning and purification. Use blue and turquoise for clearing inflamed skin. Use purple and yellow for clearing dry skin. Use indigo for clearing oily skin. Use pink to connect to love for all skin types.

Small Intestine:

The small intestines symbolises digestion and absorption of energy from others. If you have problems here you absorb too much negative energy from people around you which makes you feel vulnerable, sensitive, insecure and confused. You often sabotage yourself, procrastinate, and feel lost and abandoned. You lack personal boundaries and this keeps you unprotected and permeable, you may also suffer from unrequited love.

Healing Technique:

Tune into your intestines. Breathe deeply and slowly. Put your both hands over your belly button. Let the tips of your fingers join, all pointing away from you. Cross the thumbs. Concentrate on your small intestines. Chant the sound, "OMM" for 2-3 min and sense the vibrations of this sound in your belly.

Say: "Intuitive Healing Power, please release all insecurity, confusion, abandonment and struggle from my intestines. Please dissolve all charge and all points of view that contribute to this condition. Thank you."

Rub your hands together until they are warm. Start a downward movement over your small intestines area. Feel that your hands remove all blockages and toxicity. Do it for 2-3 minutes.

Visualise your hands are transmitting yellow lights. Transfer the yellow lights to your intestines by doing a clockwise movement over the area. Say: "Intuitive Healing Power, please instil security, confidence, strength and power into my intestines. Allow me to love and appreciate myself. Thank you."

Do the same procedure with the colour green.

Say: "Intuitive Healing Power, please heal and rejuvenate my intestines and all related organs to their maximum health and wellness. Thank you."

Before going to bed ask for a healing dream. Say: "I need to experience a dream that makes me feel safe and secure, loved and lovable. Thank you."

Emotional release: To complete the process of healing you must work on releasing stress, worry, low self-esteem, being overwhelmed and fear. Forgive yourself and others.

Colour therapy: Work with green and orange for cleaning and energising, work with yellow for strengthening.

Spine:

The spine represents support, safety and security.

Upper Part (neck area):

Experiencing a lack of emotional support in your life. Feeling that significant people in your life don't understand or support you. You may feel unloved or you may be holding back your love from someone. You may also feel that somebody is always on your back.

Middle Back (thoracic area):

Do you often scream, "Get off my back!?" Do you feel stabbed in the back? Do you carry guilt? Are you afraid to explore your past because of the fear that you may find something you keep hidden?

Lower Back (lumbar area):

Worrying about finances. The amount of money you have has nothing to do with it. It's the fear of lack of financial support, the fear of your own survival that amplifies the pain.

Sacrum:

Holding on to old anger, carrying guilt, resentment and shame, Feeling a loss of power, and engaging in self-sabotage.

Coccyx (tailbone):

Holding on to the past and "sitting on old pain." Blaming everybody, feeling betrayed and cheated, sabotaging your own success.

Healing Technique:

Tune into your back. Become aware of the emotional baggage you carry on your back. When breathing and exhaling, visualise releasing the old baggage. Feel lighter with every breath.

One way to heal your back is to massage the reflex points on the soles of your feet. Hold your foot with your hands and start massaging the inner edge of your foot from the big toe to the heel. Stroke your foot then do a circular movement with your fingers. Direct your attention to your spine, especially to the area of pain.

Say: "Intuitive Healing Power, please release all pain, tension and baggage from my back. Please dissolve all points of view that contributed to this condition. Thank you."

Repeat the word 'Clear' a few times to strengthen the intention.

Massage the area around your heel and around your ankle. Sense the painful points and notice their connection to your spine. By cleaning and energising these areas you clean and energise your spine.

Sit straight and arch your back forward and keep the tension for 5 seconds, then relax. Repeat arching and relaxing 10 times.

Then arch your back backwards, keep the tension and relax. Repeat 10 times. Feel the energy flow in your spine while doing arching and relaxing.

Say: "Intuitive Healing Power, please instil confidence, courage and self-esteem into my system. Bring all my vertebras into alignment. Thank you."

Now use hand reflexology to relieve your back pain. With your right thumb massage along the outside edge of your left palm, then switch your hands. Say: "Intuitive Healing Power, please heal and rejuvenate my spine. Thank you."

Before going to bed ask for a healing dream. Say: "I need a dream to help me heal my back and experience safety, security and Divine protection. Thank you."

Emotional release: To complete the process of healing you must work on releasing stress, worry, guilt, low self-esteem and fear. Forgive yourself and others.

Colour therapy: Work with green and orange for cleaning and energising, work with yellow for strengthening, use red for self-empowerment.

Spleen:

The spleen represents your strength and immunity. Problems here imply that you are overly sensitive, easily swayed and continuously stressing about others. You may be trying to control others or letting others control you, feeling weak, unable to face your own issues and having difficulty in expressing your true needs.

Healing Technique:

Tune into your spleen. Breathe deeply and slowly. Visualise your spleen, ask yourself, "Why do I let others control me? Do I try to control others? Who and what am I obsessed with?"

Acknowledging these truths will release blocked energy from your system.

Rub your hands together for 30 seconds until they are warm. Place your hands over your spleen and start downward sweeping movements. Visualise removing all negativity and blockages.

Say: "Intuitive Healing Power, please release all irritation, helplessness, control and frustration from my spleen. Remove all charge and all points of view that contributed to this condition. Thank you."

Repeat the word 'Clear' a few times to strengthen the intention.

Visualise your hands are transmitting orange lights. Put your hands over your spleen and transfer this orange light inside your body by doing a clockwise hand movement.

Say: "Intuitive Healing Power, please instil strength, confidence and power into my spleen. Allow me to be happy, creative and joyful. Thank you."

Breathe through your spleen and sense the subtle energy inside you. Do this for 10-15 minutes. Say: "Intuitive Healing Power, please heal and regenerate my spleen to its maximum health and wellness."

Before going to bed ask for a healing dream. Say: "I need a healing dream to make me experience the feelings of joy, peace, love and security."

Emotional release: To complete the process of healing you must work on releasing stress, worry, fear and anger. Forgive yourself and others.

Colour therapy: Work with green and orange for cleaning and energising. Work with yellow for strengthening.

Stomach:

The stomach represents digesting your life experiences. If you have problems here you have difficulty taking life as it is, procrastinating and worrying about old issues. You may be behaving in a superior and controlling way but feeling fearful and inferior inside. You have a demanding attitude but are afraid of rejection, being over-sensitive to criticism and self-obsessed. Have tendency to feel attacked and punched in the stomach.

Healing Technique:

Tune in to your stomach. Breathe deeply and slowly. Become aware of all the feelings, sensations and thoughts that are stored in your stomach. Ask, "If my stomach could talk what it would say? If my stomach could hold a memory, what memory would it be? If my stomach held a picture what would this picture would be?"

Acknowledge these truths and allow yourself to release all negative energy with each breath.

Imagine you are surrounded by a violet flame, visualise it for 3-5 minutes, then, rub your hands together for 30 seconds. Place your hands over your stomach and sense the energy they emit. Start doing a downwards sweeping motion at your stomach. Sweep all negative energy from your stomach and throw it into the violet flame.

Say: "Intuitive Healing Power, please release all frustration, control, arrogance, guilt and rejection from my stomach. Please remove all charge, negative and positive and all points of view that contribute to this condition. Thank you."

Repeat the word 'Clear' a few times to strengthen the intention.

Now, with your right hand massage the central part of your left hand. This area is energetically connected to your stomach. Then swap hands and massage the middle part of your left hand.

Say: "Intuitive Healing Power, please instil confidence, trust and self-empowerment into my stomach. Thank you. "

For 10-15 minutes continue to massage the middle part of your hand, breathe deeply through your stomach and sense the subtle energy inside you.

Say: "Intuitive Healing Power, please heal and regenerate my stomach to its maximum strength and vitality. Thank you."

Before going to bed ask for a healing dream. Say: "I want a dream that helps me experience peace, safety and relaxation."

Emotional release: To complete the process of healing you must work on releasing fear, control, rejection, attack and anger.

Colour therapy: Work with green, yellow and orange.

Teeth:

The teeth represent your capacity to bite, chew and speak. Problems here show that you are unable to communicate your personal needs and feelings. You are burdened with indecisiveness, procrastination and lack of confidence. You have a tendency to feel like a failure, give up easily and are stuck in unresolved childhood issues. You may continuously sabotage yourself and feel unsure in your life.

Healing Technique:

Tune into your teeth. Imagine you hold a magic brush which cleans all toxins, bacteria and density from your teeth. Visualise cleaning every tooth separately, one by one.

Say: "Intuitive Healing Power, please remove all shame, indecisiveness, fear, guilt and bitterness from my teeth. Please remove all charge and all points of view that contributed to this condition. Thank you."

Repeat the word 'Clear' a few times to strengthen the intention.

If you experience a toothache you can relieve it by massaging your finger knuckles (close to your nails). For right top and bottom teeth, massage the finger knuckles on your right hand. For left top and bottom teeth massage your finger knuckles on your left hand.

Press gently and tightly around the knuckle until you find a sore spot. Press it several times. Visualise the connection between your finger knuckles and your teeth.

Rub your hands together for 30 seconds. Put them slightly apart and visualise a blue light between your palms. Bring your hands to your teeth and bathe them with blue.

Say: "Intuitive Healing Power, please instil strength, clarity and confidence into my system. Allow me to speak my truth and become an empowered person. Thank you."

Breathe through your painful teeth for 5-7 minutes. Visualise releasing the pain when you exhale.

Say: "Intuitive Healing Power, please heal and regenerate my teeth to their maximum health and strength. Thank you."

Before going to bed make a request for a healing dream. Say: "I need a dream to help me experience the feelings of confidence, self-empowerment and love."

Emotional release: To complete the process of healing you must work on releasing shame, guilt, rejection, fear and anger.

Colour therapy: Work with white, blue and indigo to clean your teeth and relieve pain from them.

Testicles:

The testicles symbolise your connection to masculine power. Problems here imply that you are feeling insecure, threatened and rejecting your masculinity. You are holding onto guilt, shame and anger; unable to forgive and disconnected from your inner voice. You feel like giving up.

Healing Technique:

Become aware of who you need to forgive. Visualise this person in front of you and verbally express your feelings. Imagine there is an energy cord in your belly connecting you and this person. With your right hand do a chop like movement to disconnect and free yourself from the energy of this person. Do a chop with your left hand. Repeat 3 times with both hands. Visualise that the cord is gone.

Say: "Intuitive Healing Power, please release all negativity, guilt, shame and threats from my testicles. Allow me to forgive and let go of the past. Thank you. "

Rub your hands together for 30 seconds to energise them. Put them over your lower abdomen and start a sweeping motion. Sweep away all negative energy that is stored there.

Repeat the word 'Clear' a few times to strengthen the intention.

Visualise that your hands are transmitting orange lights. Orange is the colour of sexual power, strength and confidence. Place your hand over the lower part of your body and start a clockwise movement. Feel the energy of orange entering your lower parts.

Say: "Intuitive Healing Power, please instil confidence, strength and masculine power into my sexual organs. Allow me to feel strong, empowered and intuitive. Thank you."

Do the same process with the green colour and say: "Intuitive Healing Power, please heal and regenerate my testicles to their maximum health and vitality. Thank you."

At night, ask for a healing dream, say: "I want to experience a dream that makes me feel strong, safe and empowered. This dream will help me heal my sex organs." Write this request on a piece of paper and put it under your pillow. Record your dream first thing in the morning.

Emotional release: To complete the process of healing you must work on releasing shame, guilt, rejection, fear and anger.

Colour therapy: Work with orange and green for cleansing and energising. Work with yellow for strength and confidence.

Thalamus:

The thalamus symbolises a switchboard for your senses. Problems here imply that you are disconnected from your feelings, not understanding yourself and working against 'mother nature'. You tend to feel confused, disempowered and dishonoured; experiencing lack of clear directions and purpose in life.

Healing Technique:

Tune into your head and become aware of your own feelings. Sense the subtle energy inside your head. Say: "Intuitive Healing Power, please help me release all confusion, disconnectedness, chaos and stress from my thalamus. Please release all points of view that contribute to this condition. Thank you."

Sit on a chair or cross legged on the floor. Put your hands in front of your chest. The middle fingers are straight and touching at the tops, pointing forward. The other fingers are bended and touch at the upper two phalanges. The thumbs point towards your chest and touch at the tops. Keep this position and chant the sound 'OMM' for 5 minutes. Feel the vibrations of these sounds in your head. The vibrations of this sound harmonises your brain cells.

Say: "Intuitive Healing Power, please instil clarity, brightness, intuitive connection and wellbeing into my brain. Please allow me to live my life with grace and ease. Thank you."

Visualise a bright indigo light entering your head. Bathe your thalamus and other head structures with indigo. Say: "Intuitive Healing Power, please heal and regenerate my thalamus and all related organs to their maximum health and wellness. Thank you." Feel the vibrations of the indigo colour inside your head. Indigo can harmonise your brain and balance your senses.

Ask for a healing dream before going to bed. Say: "I want a dream the helps me heal my thalamus and brings me clarity, safety and divine support. Thank you." Record your dream first thing in the morning, and then interpret it.

Emotional release: To complete the process of healing you must work on releasing the feelings of being stuck, fear, stress and anger.

Colour therapy: Work with indigo and white for cleansing and purification. Work with yellow for strength and confidence. Work with purple for intuitive connection.

Thighs:

The thighs represent your tribal (family) connections and your sense of power. Problems here imply that you are holding onto childhood traumas, resentment and fear. You are resisting life and new ideas; feeling unloved, rejected and second best, often putting needs of others first and ignoring your own needs. You are unable to nurture yourself and take care of yourself.

Healing Technique:

Tune into your thighs, became aware of all the feelings that contribute to this condition. Ask yourself, "Who and what do I treat as more important than myself? In what way do I let myself down?" Listen to the answer...

Visualise that you are surrounded by a violet flame. Feel and sense the energy of this flame around you. With both hands pull the negativity out of your thighs. Burn it in the violet flame.

Say: "Intuitive Healing Power, please release all traumas, criticism and resentment from my thighs." Repeat the word 'Clear' a few times to strengthen the intention.

Massage your thighs. Do a stroking movement up and down from the knee to the upper thigh. Rub gently the entire thigh. Squeeze and release muscles lightly in rhythm. Give a light punch using a lightly clenched fist.

Say: "Intuitive Healing Power, please instil joy, happiness, and confidence into my thighs. Allow me to love and nurture myself. Thank you."

Tense your thighs and hold the tension for 5 seconds. Release it. Feel the difference between tension and relaxation. Repeat this 10 times. Then visualise an orange light entering your thighs, strengthening and energising them.

Say: "Intuitive Healing Power, please heal and rejuvenate my thighs to their maximum strength and vitality. Thank you. "

Ask for a healing dream before going to bed. Say: "I need a dream to heal my thighs and experience joy, love, Divine support and safety."

Emotional release: To complete the process of healing you must work on releasing guilt, rejection, fear, judgment and anger.

Colour therapy: Work with orange, green for cleansing and energising. Work with yellow for strength and confidence.

Throat:

The throat symbolises self-expression and will power. Problems show that you suffer from the inability to communicate and express your needs. You may engage in people pleasing, thinking that you are trapped in a situation or have no choice. You have problems with trusting others and yourself. You feel uninspired; you believe you lack things in your life, sabotage yourself and don't know what you want out of life.

Healing Technique:

Tune into your throat. Breathe deeply and slowly. Relax as much as you can, ask yourself: "Am I able to express myself honestly and openly when I need to? Do I follow my internal guidance or do I just try to please others in order to avoid conflict? Do I know what I want?" Acknowledging these truths will release the blocked energy out of your throat.

Rub your hands together for 30 seconds. With your right hand start a downward sweeping motion over your throat. Sweep away negative energy and throw it in the fire, a candle or an imaginary fire.

Say: "Intuitive Healing Power, please release all self-doubt, unworthiness, guilt, sadness and limitations from my throat. Please dissolve all conditioning and all points of view that contribute to this condition. Thank you."

Repeat the word 'Clear' a few times to strengthen the intention.

Sit comfortably. Cross your fingers on the inside of your hands, without the thumbs. Let the thumbs touch at the tops, and pull them slightly up. Focus on your throat. Chant the sound 'HAM'. Feel the vibration of this sound in your throat. Continue for 3-5 minutes. The vibration of this sound harmonises and balances the cells of your throat.

Say: "Intuitive Healing Power, please instil inspiration, joy, trust, happiness and clarity into my throat. Allow me to express myself clearly and freely. Thank you."

Rub your hands together for 30 seconds. Put them slightly apart and visualise a blue light between your palms. Put your hands on the throat and say: "Intuitive Healing Power, please heal and rejuvenate my throat to its maximum health and vitality. Thank you."

Before going to bed ask: "Can I have a dream that helps me heal my throat and makes me feel inspired, empowered, and guided. Thank you."

Emotional release: To complete the process of healing you must work on releasing stress, worry, rejection, fear and hurt.

Colour therapy: Work with blue, turquoise and azure.

Thymus gland:

The thymus represents immunity and protection. Problems here imply that you tend to feel like a victim, have a lack of integrity, experience difficulty moving forward and taking responsibility. You feel tired, let down and sabotaged.

Healing Technique:

Close your eyes and tune into your thymus. Sit comfortably and breathe. Become aware of all the negative feelings that contribute to this condition, visualise that with every breath out you are releasing negativity from your body. Feel lighter and lighter.

Say: "Intuitive Healing Power, please release all stress, victimhood, self-doubt, tiredness and sadness from my throat. Please dissolve all conditioning and all points of view that contribute to this condition. Thank you."

Repeat the word 'Clear' a few times to strengthen the intention.

Connect the tips of your index finger and thumb on both your hands. Put your left hand on your left knee and your right hand in front of your thymus (near your breast bone). Concentrate on your thymus.

Chant the sound 'YAM'. Feel the vibration of this sound behind your breast bone. Continue this for 3-5 minutes. This sound harmonises and balances your body cells.

Say: "Intuitive Healing Power, please instil strength, confidence and vitality into my thymus and immune system. Allow me to experience joy and love. Thank you."

Close your eyes and smile, spread the energy of your smile through your body, feel that your thymus is smiling and your whole immune system is smiling.

Say: "Intuitive Healing Power, please heal and revive my thymus and my immune system. Thank you."

Before going to bed ask for a dream. Say: "I need to experience a dream that helps me heal my thymus and makes me feel strong, powerful and inspired." Record your dream first thing in the morning.

Emotional release: To complete the process of healing you must work on releasing stress, worry, being stuck, rejection, fear and hurt.

Colour therapy: Work with orange and green for cleansing, use pink for unconditional love.

Thyroid glands:

The thyroids represent expressing your truth and following your intuition. If you have problems here you are feeling depressed, humiliated, rejected, repressed or put down. You are trying to please others and believe that you never get what you want. You are unable to say 'no' to others and feel guilty if you do. You may find yourself rushing and worrying a lot about needless things.

Healing Technique:

Tune into your thyroids. Become aware of the thoughts and feelings that contribute to this condition. Who are you trying to please? What truth are you hiding from yourself? What do you want to do in life but you don't?

Connect to your thyroids and try to retrieve some cellular memories. Ask: "If my thyroids had memories what they would be? If my thyroids stored a picture what would it be? If my thyroids stored a word what it would be?" Listen to the answers, the answers may come right away or later on, sometimes they come a few days later. The important thing is to ask and set the intention.

Now rub your hands together for 30 seconds. Put your hand over your thyroids and start a downward sweeping movement. Visualise you're removing all negativity from your thyroids.

Say: "Intuitive Healing Power, please release all tiredness, listlessness, stress and victimhood from my thyroids. Please remove all conditioning and all points of view that contribute to this condition. Thank you."

Repeat the word 'Clear' a few times to strengthen the intention.

Visualise that your hands are transmitting a blue light. Put your hands on your thyroids and bathe them with blue. Feel the vibrations of the blue colour inside your thyroids. Blue is the colour of communication and can enable you to speak your truth.

Say: "Intuitive Healing Power, please instil confidence, clear communication, self-esteem, courage, self-love and trust into my thyroids. Thank you."

Breathe deeply and slowly through your thyroids for 5-6 minutes. Feel the subtle energy inside you. Say: "Intuitive Healing Power, please heal and rejuvenate my thyroids to their maximum health and wellness. Allow me to express myself freely and creatively. Thank you."

Before going to bed ask for a healing dream. Say: "I want to experience a dream that helps me heal my thyroids and makes me connect to my internal voice and divine power. Thank you."

Emotional release: To complete the process of healing you must work on releasing stress, worry, fear guilt and hurt.

Colour therapy: Work with blue, turquoise and indigo.

Toes:

The toes stand for your direction in life. If you have problems here you feel that you are going in the wrong direction and do not belong where you are, you may want to get out of the situation and hide. You overload yourself with feelings of stress, judgement, rejection and criticism.

Right toes connect to your masculine, material or physical side. Left toes connect to your feminine, spiritual or emotional side.

Big Toe:

This toe represents your direction in life. Deviation of the big toe implies going in the wrong direction, against your dreams. A painful big toe indicates outdated beliefs about life, holding onto money and security problems. You probably have difficulty expressing yourself. On a physical level you can experience throat, teeth, gums and mouth, jaw, oesophagus, thyroid or neck problems.

Second Toe:

This toe represents feelings of love, security and belonging to a group or a cause. If you have problems here you may experience an inferiority complex and sense of not belonging, difficulty trusting, wanting to be in a different place. Physically you may also experience problems with lungs, heart, breast, and chest.

Third Toe:

This toe represents seeing your future with clarity especially in relation to your work and finances. A problem here means that you are seeing yourself as a failure, being unrealistic about work and having an unclear vision regarding your future. Physically you may also experience problems with liver, gall bladder, stomach and pancreas.

Forth Toe:

This toe represents how you feel about life. Problems here mean that you have feelings of anxiety, depression, lack of control over situations or wanting to run away from a situation. You may feel confused, unable to take responsibility for yourself. Physically you may also experience bladder, lower back, spleen and digestive problems.

Fifth Toe:

This toe represents your sense of self-worth. Problems here mean that you have suppressed aggression, rejection and are struggling. Physically you may also experience sexual problems, partnership issues, neurosis, urinary problems, low bowel disorders, vascular problems, skin issues, reproductive difficulties, depression, sciatica and headaches.

Healing Technique:

Tune into your toes. Become aware of your feelings that contribute to this problem. Hold your foot, look at your toes. With your hand gently pull the negative energy from each toe and throw it into the fire, a candle or an imaginary fire.

Say: "Intuitive Healing Power, please release all negativity from my toes. Thank you." Repeat the word 'Clear' a few times to strengthen the intention.

Massage your toes and visualise bathing them with a particular colour. The choice of colour depends on the chakra connected to each toe.

First toe connects to the 5th (throat) chakra: Blue colour.
Second toe connects to the 4th (heart) chakra: Green colour.
Third toe connects to the 3rd (solar plexus) chakra: Yellow colour.
Fourth toe connects to the 2nd (relationship) chakra: Orange colour.
Fifth toe connects to the 1st (tribal, family) chakra: Red colour.

Say: "Intuitive Healing Power, please heal and regenerate my toe. Allow me to go in the right direction throughout my life and feel strong and confident. Thank you."

Emotional release: To complete the process of healing you must work on releasing relevant emotions for each toe.

Colour therapy: Work with the relevant colour for each toe.

Tongue:

The tongue represents speaking your truth. Problems here imply that you are not speaking your truth and trying to please others instead. You may be gossiping, judging and criticising others, saying that things are OK while they are not; feeling inferior and unable to stand up for yourself.

Healing Technique:

Tune into your tongue. Become aware of your thoughts and feelings. Open your mouth and protrude your tongue. Look in the mirror to see your tongue, notice what colour, shape and consistency it has, run your tongue around your lips slowly in circles. Do it 10 times.

Run your tongue round the inside of your mouth, push it between your lips, up round the outside of your teeth, over the roof of your mouth and down on the base of your mouth. Do this 10 times.

Feel the sensation you have on your tongue after doing the movements. Say: "Intuitive Healing Power, please help me release the feelings of fear, criticism, judgement and inferiority. Let me speak my truth with confidence. Thank you."

Take a deep breath and exhale through your tongue. Sense the energy inside your tongue.

Now, say 'lah lah lah lah lah lah lah' ......at an easy speed. Do this for 10 seconds, feeling the tip of your tongue curl up behind your top teeth.

In front of a mirror protrude your tongue and look at it, giving it your complete attention. Notice if your tongue looks any firmer than it did before the exercises. The changes may be minimal and not easy to see, but with close attention you can spot the difference.

Say: "Intuitive Healing Power, please instil truth and confidence into my tongue. Let me speak gracefully and honestly. Thank you."

Relax your tongue. Visualise an orange light enters your mouth and heals it. Say: "Intuitive Healing Power, please heal and rejuvenate my tongue and mouth. Thank you."

Ask for a healing dream. Say: "I want to experience a dream that will empower me to speak my truth and make me feel loving, graceful and confident. Thank you."

Emotional release: To complete the process of healing you must work on releasing criticism, judgment, stress, fear and hurt.

Colour therapy: Work with orange and green for cleaning and energising. Use white for purification.

Tonsils:

The tonsils represent your emotional barriers and your capacity to process emotions. If you have problems here you have tried to repress your emotions in order to keep peace with others. You are not expressing your creativity and not speaking your truth, you worry about not being accepted.

Healing Technique:

Tune into your tonsils. Acknowledge the emotions you have been suppressing. What feelings and thoughts are you hiding inside? What would you like to say out loud but you don't? Whom would you like to say it to?

Open your mouth and look at your tonsils. Notice their colour, shape, consistency and size. Take a glass of warm water and add a tea spoon of baking soda. Stir the solution until it becomes white. Gargle with this solution and visualise that you are purifying your tonsils with a white colour.

Sense the difference in sensations before and after gargling.

Say: "Intuitive Healing Power, please release all hurts, fear, difficulty expressing myself, criticism and judgement from my tonsils. Thank you."

Repeat the word 'Clear' a few times to enhance the intention.

Rub your hands together for 30 seconds. Put one of your hands in front of your throat and start a downward sweeping motion. Sweep away all negative energy from your tonsils and throat.

Visualise your hands are transmitting a blue light. Do clockwise movements with your hand in front of your throat putting the blue energy inside.

Say: "Intuitive Healing Power, please instil confidence, strength and creativity into my tonsils and throat. Allow me to express my needs clearly and confidently. Thank you."

Do the same process with a green colour. Say: "Intuitive Healing Power, please heal and purify my tonsils. Thank you."

Ask for a healing dream before going to bed. Say: "Can I have a dream that helps me experience peace, harmony and balance in my whole being and allows me to speak my needs and feelings easily and confidently."

Emotional release: To complete the process of healing you must work on releasing criticism, judgment, anger, stress and hurt.

Colour therapy: Work with orange and blue for cleaning and energising. Use white for purification.

Uterus:

The uterus represents your creativity and femininity. When you have problems you are feeling disconnected from your feminine side, not expressing your creativity, not listening to your intuition. You are not loving towards yourself and not nurturing yourself enough. You feel like giving up and need constant approval of others in order to do things.

Healing Technique:

Close your eyes and ask yourself, "Who am I trying to please? Whose approval do I need? In what way do I block my creativity?" Acknowledging these truths will release some blocked energy from your uterus.

Now, tune into your uterus. With your mind's eye explore the organ. Visualise the negativity inside your uterus as weeds. With your hand pull out the weeds from your uterus and throw the 'weeds' into the fire, a candle or an imaginary fire.

Say: "Intuitive Healing Power, please remove all hurts, rejection, unfairness and disappointments from my uterus. Please release all charge, positive and negative and all points of view that contribute to this problem. Thank you."

Rub your hands together for 30 seconds. Separate them slightly and visualise orange lights between your palms. Put your hand in front of your uterus and start a clockwise movement. Visualise you are nourishing and energising the area with a bright orange light.

Say: "Intuitive Healing Power, please instil balance, femininity, creativity, joy, happiness and power into my uterus. Thank you"

Breathe through the organ and sense its subtle energy. Continue to visualise the orange light rejuvenating and repairing your uterus from the inside.

Say: "Intuitive Healing Power, please heal and strengthen my uterus to its maximum capacity. Thank you."

Before going to bed ask for a healing dream. Say: "I need a dream that helps me heal my uterus and makes me feel feminine, creative and happy. Thank you."

Emotional release: To complete the process of healing you must work on releasing guilt, shame, rejection, sadness, stress and hurt.

Colour therapy: Work with orange and yellow for cleaning, energising and strengthening. Use pink for love.

Vagina:

The vagina represents femininity. A problem here means that you are disconnected from your feminine side and holding onto anger with the opposite sex, carrying sexual guilt and punishing yourself. You try to please others but deny your own needs, feel unattractive, unlovable and as a victim. You tend to reject pleasures in life and experience fear of intimacy.

Healing Technique:

Tune into your vagina. Sense the energy inside it. To heal your vagina you need to be able to embrace your femininity and enjoy being a woman. Ask yourself, "How much do you love being a woman? What do you feel about your sexuality? Do you like it or do you feel guilty about it? Where does this guilt come from? What do you feel about making love? What does your mother and sisters think about sexuality? How openly can you discuss this subject with them?"

Don't judge your answers and don't dwell on them. Just by acknowledging these truths will release some blocked energy from your system and you will start to feel lighter.

Embracing your sensuality can also help you heal. This means you should get pleasure in what you sense: What you feel, smell, hear, see and touch. Try to engage in creative activities that bring you joy and stimulate your senses: Dancing, singing, painting, writing poetry or designing. Healing your femininity is associated with beginning to create and experiencing joy from doing it. Start doing this today.

Now sit comfortably and breathe deeply. Keep sensing the energy in your vagina. Visualise when you exhale, you are releasing all negativity from the organ.

Say: "Intuitive Healing Power, please remove all anger, hurts, rejection and disappointments from my vagina. Please release all charge and all points of view that contribute to this condition. Thank you."

Rub your hands together for 30 seconds. Separate them slightly apart and visualise a beautiful pink light between your palms. Place your hand over your reproductive organs and start a clockwise movement to put pink energy in.

Say: "Intuitive Healing Power, please instil joy, playfulness, femininity, creativity and love into my vagina. Thank you."

Now visualise green lights coming from your palms. Keep your hands over your reproductive organs and continue a clockwise movement.

Say: "Intuitive Healing Power, please heal and rejuvenate my vagina and reproductive organs to their maximum strengths and vitality. Thank you."

Before going to bed ask for a healing dream. Say: "I want a dream that makes me feel loving, happy, joyful, feminine and creative. The loving energy of these feelings will help me heal my vagina."

Emotional release: To complete the process of healing you must work on releasing guilt, shame, anger, rejection, sadness, stress and hurt.

Colour therapy: Work with orange, green and yellow for cleaning, energising and strengthening. Use pink and magenta for love and inspiration.

Veins:

The veins stand for circulating joy and love inside your body. Problems imply that you are disconnected from love and nurturing. Varicose veins mean that you are standing in a situation you hate, feeling blocked, discouraged, over-worked, overburdened and underappreciated. Blocked veins means you are holding on to guilt, shame, rejection, outdated beliefs and focusing on the negative side.

Healing Technique:

Relax by taking a few deep breaths. Tune into your veins, ask yourself: "Where do I compromise myself? What am I holding onto? What thoughts and behaviours are keeping me stuck?"

Take a piece of paper and draw a vertical line down the middle of it. On the left side write down negative behaviours that keep you stuck. On the right side, write down what life changes you need to implement to stop them. Every day look at this list and remind yourself what has to be done. Continue this for 3 weeks.

Now tune into your body. Breathe deeply. Visualise with every breath you are releasing burdens and toxins out of your system, observe a dark cloud leaving your body.

Say: "Intuitive Healing Power, please release all guilt, shame, discouragement, burdens, anger, hurts and rejection from my veins. Please take away all charge, positive and negative and all points of view that contribute to this condition. Thank you."

Repeat the word 'Clear' a few times to enhance the intention.

Visualise a silver light entering your vascular system. Silver clears and repairs veins. Bathe your vascular system with silver.

Say: "Intuitive Healing Power, please instil clarity, strength and power into my veins. Help me to re-connect to my intuition and let love and joy to circulate freely through my veins. Thank you."

Visualise a green light entering your vascular system, healing and restoring it.

Say: "Intuitive Healing Power, please repair and strengthen my veins to their maximum health and vitality. Thank you."

Emotional release: To complete the process of healing you must work on releasing guilt, shame, anger, criticism, judgement, stress and hurt.

Colour therapy: Work with silver, green and blue for clearing veins. Use red for strength and power.

Wrist:

The wrists represent movement and ease. If you have problems you feel stressed, stuck, overworked and irritated. You tend to control things, hold on to old limiting beliefs about relationships and money.

Healing Technique:

Sit, relax and take a few deep breaths. Shake your hands as if you are trying to shake off problems from your wrists. Tune into your wrists and sense the energy inside them, ask yourself: "What chains am I wearing around my wrists? Who or what am I trying to control?" Listen to the answers...

Shake your wrists again and visualise you are shaking off all chains, limitations and pain.

Say: "Intuitive Healing Power, please release all burdens, anger, hurts, righteousness and control from my wrists. Please take away all charge, positive and negative and all points of view that contribute to this problem. Thank you."

Repeat the word 'Clear' a few times to enhance the intention.

Rub your hands together for 30 seconds. Put your hands slightly apart and visualise a pink light between them. Close your eyes and with your left hand grip your right wrist, bathe it with pink light. Visualise your right wrists as free, healthy and light, sense the energy of the pink colour in your right wrist.

Say: "Intuitive Healing Power, please instil a sense of freedom, lightness, ease, grace and harmony into my wrists. Thank you."

Change your hands and grip your left wrist. Bathe your left wrist with pink and say: "Intuitive Healing Power, please heal and regenerate my wrists to their maximum strength and mobility. Thank you."

Ask for a healing dream. Say: "I need to experience a dream to experience the feelings of ease, grace and movement."

Emotional release: To complete the process of healing you must work on releasing stress, fear, control, criticism, judgement and hurt.

Colour therapy: Work with yellow and green for clearing. Use pink for love.

Chapter 6
The Energetic/ Emotional Meaning of Illnesses

In this chapter you will find probable psychosomatic causes of physical and mental illnesses, symptoms and conditions, which I have collected from the time I studied Psychoneuroimmunology in Russia. Since then, I have read many scientific documents that have proven these connections to be correct. You can find the bibliography of my research at the end of this book.

Every disease and disorder feeds on thoughts and emotions, their energies continue to degenerate your body on a physical level. When you understand what energies created a problem, you can release them and start to heal.

You will also discover that our bodies are trying very hard to teach us about our life, our jobs, our relationships and our attitudes to life. All our aches and pains, feelings and emotions show us that something isn't working within our body. Their purpose is to attract our attention to the problem, what they are saying is, "Stop! Listen! Change your track. Something you're doing is wrong and you need to change in order to heal."

Through my work with patients I have realised that certain emotional and spiritual issues correspond quite specifically to problems in certain parts of the body. For instance, people with heart disease have had life experiences that led them to block out intimacy or love from their lives. People with lower back pain have had persistent financial worries; people with cancer often have unresolved connections with the past, unfinished business and emotional issues; people with blood disorders frequently have deep-seated conflicts with their families of origin.

When you understand your emotional/energetic blocks and limitations you can begin to release them, and this is what this chapter is about.

Remember to use this information as a guide. Not every destructive feelings and patterns listed here will relate to you. To get more specific answers you should tune into your body and ask your intuition for help and guidance.

I recommend that you use this chapter as a cross-reference between the different sections. First, read about the illness or symptom and become aware of what emotions and feelings are related to you. Second, release these emotions following the technique's described in the "The Secret Energy of Your Emotions" chapter.

You can also heal any of your problems using the 7 steps to intuitive healing which we have discussed in the previous chapters.

I also must warn you that all these techniques are not a replacement for a healthy diet, regular exercise and appropriate healthcare from your medical practitioner. These techniques are designed to provide additional support to allow your body to become healthy, stronger and vibrant. These techniques will help you to ignite your own intuitive healing power and make your body begin to heal itself.

I strongly believe that healing is always possible. Even if your wounds are deep or illness is severe – it's possible to release long-held fears and negative thoughts toward oneself and others. This kind of energetic release and healing can occur even though one's body may be dying physically.

Healing is a natural process and it always comes from within. Healing is different from curing, though curing and the restoration of physical function often accompany healing.

To sum up, the emotional explanations regarding symptoms and illnesses in this chapter will help you bring meaning to your pain, and by bringing meaning to your pains and illnesses you can be guided to heal.

To heal your problems, follow the 7 Steps to Intuitive Healing:
Step 1: Tune into your body.
Step 2: Sense the subtle energy in your body.
Step 3: Visualise the structure of your body.
Step 4: Ask your intuition for help and guidance.
Step 5: Manipulate the energy with your hands.
Step 6: Use the energy of colours to counteract the problem.
Step 7: Listen to your dreams and visions.

A

Abdominal Cramps

Feeling stuck in a situation you don't like and can't see a way out of this. Experiencing tension, gripping, holding onto the 'same old, same old' pattern. Can't let go of stress and fear. Blaming and criticising yourself.

Abscess

Bottling up anger and feeling hurt. Holding onto frustration, irritation and criticism; wanting revenge. There is something painful you keep inside that must be expressed and released.

Accidents

Feeling overwhelmed by the negative mind: Angry, arrogant and fearful. Wanting to rebel against authority; believing in pain and punishment, experiencing inner conflict.

Acid Reflux

Not liking your situation and wanting to find the way out. Blaming yourself for the past choices and having doubts about your actions. Resisting life and holding onto the past.

Acne
Feeling uncomfortable in your own skin. Feeling unloved, rejected and unworthy. Engaging in self-hatred and self-sabotage; believing in pain and punishment.

Acrophobia
Fear of falling down. Feeling unsupported and unprotected.

Addiction
Trying to numb the pain, stress and anxiety. Self-hate, self-rejection, self-sabotage. Running away from life, not wanting to face life experiences.

Addison's Disease
Too much stress, worries and anxiety. Always busy and having no time for rest. Pushing things and resisting the natural flow of life. Denying your joy, fun and happiness.

Adenoids
Difficulty expressing your own needs due to family friction and arguments. Feeling unwelcomed, unsupported, unloved.

Aging (fear of)
Holding on to the old way of thinking and wrong social beliefs about aging. Not listening to your own intuition. Wanting things to stay the same and resisting the natural flow of life.

Agoraphobia
Fear of losing control, not trusting others and thinking people take advantage of you. Feeling like a victim and holding on to internal struggle, hopelessness and helplessness.

AIDS
Feeling guilty, hopeless, helpless, defenseless and dirty. Denial of the self, carrying sexual shame.

Alcoholism

Self-rejection, bottled up anger and hurt. Feelings of futility, inadequacy, stagnation, boredom and depression. Disconnectedness from the soul. Wanting to numb painful thoughts, feelings and hide from the world.

Allergy

Irritated and annoyed with your tribe. Losing your own power and thinking that others are on your back. Carrying unresolved childhood traumas. Experiencing emotional overload and lack of boundaries. Withholding love and kindness.

Alzheimer's Disease

Wanting to forget the past. Refusal to see the world as it is. Too much suppressed emotions that eat you away. Feeling lost, confused and unimportant.

Amenorrhea

Uncomfortable with your femininity. Holding resentment against your mother or sister. Feeling abandoned, not worthy, not loved, empty. Losing your power as a woman. Lack of self-nurturing.

Amnesia

Wanting to forget the past. Feeling unhappy, unfulfilled and repressed. Having difficulty to forgive.

Anemia

You forgot how to enjoy life. Feeling deprived, lonely and separate from others. A lack of pleasure, a lack of interest in life and fear of the future. Resisting life rather than letting it to unfold. Suffering from family problems.

Anal Abscess

Having too many repressed fears. Feeling as a victim, ashamed, guilty and holding onto the past. Thinking of injustice and wanting revenge. Denying your own feelings and lying to yourself.

Anal Bleeding
Forcing things to happen rather than letting them happen. Resisting life and wanting things to be different. Refusing to take responsibility for self-created issues. Trying to control the uncontrollable, can't let go of the past, difficulty forgiving yourself and others.

Aneurism
Too much stubbornness and resistance to change. Wanting things to be your way and having too much pride to ask for help and support. Not liking where you are and needing to get out. Futile workaholic.

Angina
Lack of intimacy in relationships. Too much righteousness, not enough love and nurturing, critical, judgemental. Believing in pain and punishment.

Anorexia
Extreme denial of self-love, self-nourishment, self-nurturing and living in continuous fear. Carrying family problems and hiding them inside. Feeling rejected, not belonging and wanting to escape. Disconnected from intuition and unable to communicate your needs.

Anxiety
Living in the past or in the future, denying the now. Not trusting in the flow of life. Feeling insecure, vulnerable and helpless, focusing on the negativity, the inability to let go and forgive.

Appendicitis
Fear of losing power. Dissatisfied and disappointed with the results. Blocking the flow of good and engaging with too much thinking. Not having enough joy and pleasure.

Arteriosclerosis
Resisting life and experiencing too much tension and thinking. Feeling disconnected from your heart and intuition. Focusing on being right rather than being loved, a lack of intimacy in

relationships, pushing things to happen rather than letting them unfold naturally.

Arthritis
Too much criticising and judging. Feeling unloved, bitter, resentful, isolated and having difficulty forgiving and letting go. Being stuck in a rigid thinking pattern and not wanting to change.

Asperger's Syndrome
Can't fit in. Feeling isolated, lonely and different. Unable to communicate your feelings and needs. Looking aggressive but what you really have is a hidden desire for love and attention.

Asthma
Feeling smothered, vulnerable, stifled and suffocated. Trying to please others and often putting yourself second. Unable to say 'no' to others and allowing them to control your life. Keeping emotional burdens in your chest and suppressing them.

Astigmatism
Disliking what you see. Focusing on fears rather than seeing the full picture. Not seeing the self.

Athlete's Foot
Irritated, annoyed and angry with others. Carrying unresolved childhood issues. Feeling blocked and unloved.

Attention Deficit Disorder
Feeling trapped in your own environment. Experiencing difficulty fitting in and unable to communicate your own feelings and needs. Suppressed anger.

Autism
Feeling isolated, imprisoned, frustrated and helpless. Fear of being humiliated, laughed at and unaccepted. Stressed by your own

dependency on others. Wanting to get out of the cell and express your own creativity.

B

Bacterial Infection
Craving for attention of others, neediness and attachment to people. Hiding emotions inside rather than expressing them. Not speaking your truth. Feeling frustrated, irritated and weak.

Bad Breath
Feeling frustrated, rejected, irritated and uncomfortable with yourself. Wanting to keep people away because of the difficulty fitting in.

Baldness
Holding on to fear and tension. Trying to control life and not trusting the natural flow of life. Pushing, resisting and trying to manipulate things. Wanting to have everything your way and feeling disappointed with others.

Bed Wetting
Feeling scared of some family members or authorities. Thinking of punishment, loss of control.

Bell's Palsy
Experiencing too much strain, resisting and pushing rather than going with the flow. Bottled up anger, frustration and disappointments. Stuck in old thinking patterns and refusing to change. Wearing a mask to hide your true self and stopping the natural flow of events.

Bi-polar Disorder (Manic Depression)
Repressed childhood issues. Feeling traumatised, stressed, unbalanced and wanting to be somewhere else rather than where you are.

Experiencing too much anger and aggression towards people close to you. Wanting to break free from situations, feeling that something else controls you. Disconnected from your inner self and from the natural flow of life.

Birth Defects

Karmic choice to teach parents lessons of love, humility and compassion.

Blackheads (Pimples)

Angry with yourself and others, uncomfortable being yourself.

Bladder Cancer

Experiencing internal conflict with who you are and what you are doing in life. Keeping inside too much sadness. Holding onto guilt and clinging to the past. You are irritated with people close to you and having someone in your life who you must forgive, and let go all the feelings associated with this person.

Bleeding

Letting your joy run away from you. Sabotaging yourself. Believing that in order to achieve you must sacrifice and suffer. Focusing on negativity and on why things can't be done. Resisting life, bursting with unexpressed feelings.

Bleeding Gums

Inability to express your needs and feelings. Not speaking your truth. Unsure of yourself and hiding negativity inside. Stuck in an old pattern and not wanting to change. Extremely demanding and critical of yourself and others.

Blindness

Not wanting to see the world around you. Not liking where you are and resisting things. Too much thinking and rationalising rather than sensing and feeling.

Blisters
Pushing over your limit and not listening to your body. Experiencing lack of self-love and self-nurturing.

Bloating
Holding on to anger, self-doubting, blame, self-sabotage. Not knowing what to do next. Feeling uncomfortable with where you are. Believing you are not good enough. Thinking you must struggle in order to achieve.

Blood Clotting
Resisting the flow of life. Believing in limitations, pain and punishment. Too many disappointments and regrets.

Blood Pressure
See hypertension and hypotension

Body Odor
Dislike of the self. Fear of being yourself. Feeling rejected, isolated, mocked, unaccepted and unloved. Criticising and judging yourself.

Boils
Internal resentment and unexpressed anger. Feeling that life is unfair. Trying to control others or let yourself be controlled. Blaming others. Inability to accept yourself.

Bone Cancer
Holding on to pain, resentment, and childhood problems. Trying to rebel against authority and struggling with family issues. Not liking where you are and wanting out. Feeling that you can't stand the pain and pressure anymore, blaming yourself for the past choices. Struggling to survive.

Bone Deformity

Going against your beliefs and following wrong directions. Denying your truth for the sake of pleasing others. Feeling betrayed, hopeless and helpless. Struggling to survive.

Bone Morrow Problems

Loss of faith and directions in life. Disappointed with yourself and others. Feeling insecure, helpless, and hopeless and having fears about the future. Trying to please others to get their approval. Too clingy and needy. Family problems.

Bone Break

Reaching a breaking point in your life. Stressed and overworked beyond your limits. Believing that you need to be punished. Not honouring yourself. Feeling abused, unappreciated, unloved. Lack of nurturing and care.

Bone Weakness

Feeling unsupported, weak, unsure, limited. Giving away your power to others. Not trusting yourself and stuck in victimhood. Too sensitive to criticisms and remarks of others. Carrying too much stress, hurt, sadness and worry in your bones. Not looking after yourself and wanting someone to take care of you.

Brain Tumor

Experiencing internal conflict and stuck in negative thinking. Confused, lost, doubtful, and unstable. Not knowing who to trust. Blaming yourself for the past mistakes. Feeling trapped with no way out.

Breast Cancer

Lack of self-love, self-nurturing and self-appreciation. Continuously taking care of others and ignoring yourself. Feeling like a victim and carrying guilt and shame inside. Lack of self-confidence.

Breast Cysts/Lumps

Lack of self-nurturing. Feeling burdened by past hurts. Regretting choices once made. Feeling unsupported and un-loved by people. Holding onto sadness about how things turned out.

Breastfeeding (inability)

Feeling inadequate in a current situation. Disempowered, burdened and stressed about being a mother. Blaming and criticising yourself. Losing your own power. Trying to control people or letting yourself be controlled by others.

Bronchitis

Carrying family conflicts inside your chest. Irritated with people close to you. Blaming others for self-inflicted problems. Needing nurturing, love and care.

Bruises

Believing in pain and punishment. Blaming yourself for past mistakes. Unresolved conflicts with yourself and others.

Bulimia

Self-denial, self-punishment, self-loathing and self-sabotage. Difficulty in receiving love and nurturing. Trying to control life. Overwhelmed by negative energies from others and feeling that you must purge them to free yourself. Using food to numb your feelings and deny your intuitions.

Bunions

Feeling that you are following the wrong direction in life and making choices that limited your growth. Regretting the past and resisting change. Experiencing lack of strength and power to move forward. Unhappy with where you are.

Burns

Feeling burning up inside, being impatient and wanting things too quickly. Angry with somebody close to you.

Burping/Belching

Feeling limited, burdened, not free. Experiencing challenges in your relationship but trying to deny it. Stuck in self-limitation. Feeling unworthy of good things. Overwhelmed by stress.

Bursitis

Stuck in an old pattern. Having internal conflict and even wanting to hit someone. A lot of repressed anger. Feeling bored, uninspired and dissatisfied.

C

Callus Formation

Becoming hard on yourself. Fear solidified. Fearing your intuitions and not taking empowering actions. Resisting your own feelings. Getting stuck with limited concepts and ideas. Giving advice to others but not taking advice yourself.

Cancer

Carrying deep hurt and longstanding resentment. Feeling guilt, shame and doubt. Internal conflict with who you are and who you should be. Holding onto a deep secret or grief that eats away at you. Not loving yourself. Trying to please others. In constant need of approval.

Candida

Feeling frustrated, scattered, demanding and untrusting in your relationship. Blaming and criticising. Not willing to change.

Canker Sores

Inability to speak for yourself. Insecure, unsafe, unconfident. Experiencing self-doubt and procrastination. Feeling regretful and frustrated. Blaming and criticising yourself and others.

Carpal Tunnel Syndrome

Doing what you don't want to do. Feeling overworked, not appreciated and not valued. Suppressed anger and frustrations at life's seeming injustices. Believing in struggle, pain and punishment. Holding on to continuous strain and stress. Inability to let go.

Car Sickness

Fear of losing control. Feeling obligated, trapped and confused.

Cataracts

Seeing too many obstacles in life and a dark future. Unable to see reality from a positive side. Loss of joy and excitement. Feeling burdened by past problems, and fearing the future. No clarity in life.

Cellulite

Feeling unstable, uncertain and doubtful. Believing in age and struggle. Unexpressed anger towards yourself and others. Resisting life rather than going with the flow.

Cerebral Palsy

Needing love and affection from family. Wanting to express yourself through family love and understanding.

Cervical Cancer

Feeling uncomfortable with your femininity. Carrying some deep resentment and hurt from past relationships. Stuck in the past. Feeling ignored, unloved, betrayed, wronged and empty. Can't forgive.

Chest Congestion

Letting people control your life. Feeling smothered and suffocated. No freedom. Difficulty expressing what you want. Bottled up anger and resentment. Porous, get easily affected by other people's energy.

Chicken Pox

Feeling irritated, annoyed, unappreciated, used and unnoticed. Not belonging, disappointed with life. Needing attention. Craving for affection and love from others.

Childhood Diseases
Feeling upset, left out, unsure how to deal with life. Wanting attention and love. Believing in punishment for bad behaviour. Fear of parental fighting. Absorbing negative energy from parents.

Chills
Uncomfortable about a situation. Internal conflict, indecisiveness, desire to retreat and pull away.

Chlamydia
Feeling rejected, ashamed, used, unvalued. Allowing people to control you. Thinking that there is something wrong with you. Uncomfortable with your sexuality.

Cholesterol
Feeling insecure, vulnerable and unprotected. Constantly expecting something bad to happen. Continuous fight and flight reaction. Lack of rest, joy, self-nurturing, self-love, self-appreciation. Holding on to past hurts. Inability to let go and forgive.

Chronic Fatigue Syndrome
Losing your own power. Thinking that someone else has all the answers. Feeling vulnerable, frustrated and weak. Unable to say 'no'. Not liking life and wanting to be somewhere else. Feeling stuck in old beliefs and resisting change. Believing in struggle, pain and punishment. Feeling unworthy, unloved, unsupported.

Chronic Illness
Not feeling safe in this world. Stuck in old beliefs, refusing to change. Needing the illness and feeling comfortable with not being well. Feeling you are a victim and having strong attachment to past hurts. Not wanting to participate in life. Giving up. Inability to let go and forgive.

Circulation Problems
Unable to express your emotions in a constructive way. Stuck in an old pattern, feeling restricted and limited. Blaming and criticising others. Fear of trying new things and taking risks. Not expressing your creativity. Holding onto old wounds.

Claustrophobia
Imprisoned in your own little world. Anxious, obsessive, controlling, trying to control the uncontrollable. Perfectionism. Pushing and resisting. Believing in physical force rather than divine flow.

Cluster Headaches
Feeling attacked and criticised. Thinking too much. Suppressing anger, rejection, and disappointments. Believing in physical force rather than divine flow. Wanting to be right rather than loved and loving.

Coeliac Disease
Very sensitive, vulnerable and easily irritated. Focusing on negatives and why things can't be done. Disempowered and disconnected. Fear of criticism and rejection.

Colds
Overwhelmed, stressed, scattered. Refusing to listen to your own body. Too much to do, not taking a rest. Distracting yourself with superficial things rather than listening to your own body.

Cold Sores
Inability to express your own emotions and needs. Bottled up anger, irritability, disappointments. Allowing others to control you. Not taking charge and responsibility for yourself. Trying to please others for approval.

Colic
Feeling irritated, stressed, scattered. Too much on your plate. Craving for attention and love.

Colitis
Stuck in the past. Can't let go of the old hurts. Feeling worthless and defeated. Overwhelmed with too many emotions. Can't handle life anymore. Great need for approval of others. Lack of self-love and self-acceptance.

Coma
Wanting to escape from life. Can't take it anymore. Fear of the future.

Compulsive Eating
Trying to numb painful emotions. Do not want to feel anymore. Eating away guilt, shame, frustration, hurts. Needing attention and approval of others. Fear of failure. Struggling for control.

Constipation
Stuck in an old way of thinking. Resisting life and creative flow. Pushing and forcing rather than letting things unfold. Wanting to be right. Holding onto fear and anger. Extremely demanding, self-righteous, self-obsessed, and selfish. Fear of future.

Convulsions
Internal conflict with your dark side. Trying to control and force rather than allowing things to happen. Repressed anger. Unexpressed emotions.

Corns
Being hard on yourself. Resisting the natural flow of life. Fear of moving forward. Lack of clarity. Blaming yourself for past choices. Trying to please others for approval.

Cough
Overwhelmed with stress that comes from other people. Trying to cough up negative energy. Feeling smothered and suffocated. Self-critical. Blaming yourself and others for past choices. Lack of self-love and nurturing.

Cramps
Too much stress and struggle. Fear of future. Can't relax and let go. Distracting yourself rather than listening to your own body. Impatient, demanding, wanting things immediately. Tired and needing rest.

Crohn's Disease
Very negative attitude to life. Cynical. Critical and judgmental. Portraying to be confident on the outside while crying for help on the inside. Family problems. Hiding your own feelings and burying them rather than expressing and releasing them.

Crying
Releasing your emotions. If you are able to acknowledge your suppressed feelings crying is healing. Tears wash out negativity from inside.

Cushing's Syndrome
Overwhelmed by stress. Giving up. Believing that life is too hard and there is no help. Feeling like a victim.

Cystic Fibrosis
Thinking that life is too difficult. Believing that nobody can help and you can't thrive on your own. Stuck in victimhood. Self-rejection. Feeling unworthy and inferior.

Cyst
Believing that you can't fulfil your dreams. Holding onto past hurts and can't move forward. Doubtful about your future. Allowing other people to control your life. Feeling rejected and disappointed.

D

Dandruff
Trying to please other people. Not listening and not following your inner voice. Irritated, annoyed and disappointed with others.

Deafness
Not liking what you hear. Saying, "I don't want to hear this." Being stubborn. Holding onto old ways of thinking. Resisting change. Thinking that other people don't appreciate you and don't want to hear what you have to say. Feeling rejected.

Dementia
Can't deal with life anymore. Fears related to safety and security.

Depression
Stuck in victimhood. Losing your power and energy rapidly. Having a "I don't care anymore" attitude. Thinking that somebody else has all the answers and can save you. Not trusting yourself. Lack of spiritual connection, maybe even in a spiritual crisis craving for a better meaning to life. Ignoring and denying your intuition. Blaming yourself and others. Stuck in old ways of thinking. Resisting change.

Depression Postnatal
Feeling separated, detached, empty, abandon and overwhelmed. Can't cope with extra responsibilities. Holding onto old hurts. Stuck in limitations and guilt. Lack of trust, safety and security.

Dermatitis
Uncomfortable in your own skin. Feeling irritated, frustrated, unsatisfied. Lots of suppressed anger which is pushed through the skin. Unhappy with yourself. Lack of self-love and self-nurturing. Crying for help.

Diabetes Type 1

Craving for sweetness and attention. Trying to be indispensable to others and people please in order to get approval. Controlling people or letting yourself be controlled by others. Feeling insecure and unsure of yourself. Allow negative voices to dominate your mind.

Diabetes Type 2

Needing to control people and situations. Pushing and resisting rather than allowing things to happen. Wanting love from others but believing that you are unworthy of love. Carrying lots of guilt and shame. Believing that you must struggle to survive. Often find yourself in co-dependent relationship with nowhere to go. Stuck in a limited world of self-imprisonment.

Diarrhea

Regretting your own decisions. Feeling helpless and unsupported. Experiencing fear and anxiety. Blaming yourself.

Diverticulitis

Losing hope and sabotaging yourself. Feeling like you have no choice and nowhere to go. Stuck and imprisoned. Holding onto negativity and guilt. Thinking "what's the point?"

Dizziness

Feeling unbalanced, scattered, stressed. The body is overwhelmed. Not liking where you are. Scared and uncomfortable, wanting out, lack of inner balance and calmness.

Down Syndrome

A karmic choice to come here to teach parents unconditional love, acceptance, kindness and humility.

Drug Addictions

Escaping from life's difficulties. Not knowing how to cope. Wanting to numb the feelings. Holding onto old hurts. Hiding guilt, shame and frustration with life. Spiritual disconnectedness.

Duodenal Problems
Stuck in limited ways of thinking. Can't let go. Difficulty communicating your own needs and expressing you truth. Overwhelmed with too much going on at once. Fear of the future.

Dysentery
Your body is rebelling. Something needs to change. You have lost your connections with your inner voice. You stop growing and empowering yourself. Feeling hopeless and powerless.

Dyslexia
Wanting to do things your own way. Not living up to parental standards and being humiliated for this. Desire to express your soul by different means. Feeling misunderstood by others.

E

Earache
Not wanting to listen to your own inner voice. Not listening to others. Stuck in blame and judgments. Fear of letting others control you. Feeling ignored, unnoticed, unappreciated, stressed.

Eclampsia
Fear of the future and extra responsibilities. Thinking that you are losing your freedom. Feeling insecure, unsafe, unsupported, threatened. Believing that you have no choice. Burdened, scared and powerless. Doubting about being a good mother and providing for a new baby.

Eczema
Bottled up anger, frustration and self-rejection. Feeling second best, inferior and unaccepted. Holding onto old ways of thinking, becoming stagnant. Resisting life.

Edema
Holding onto unresolved past issues, not forgiving. Trying to hide and deny difficulties rather than facing them. Anxious,

stressed, vulnerable and not confident. Can't move forward, fear of the future.

Emphysema
Believing that life is a struggle. Denying joy, happiness and pleasure. Holding onto guilt, hurt, and stress. Anticipating bad things will happen. Extremely negative outlook. Too much thinking and not enjoying the present moment. Absorbing negativity like a sponge.

Encephalitis (viral)
Listening to the negative mind which leads to more negativity and frustration. Regretting the past or fearing the future. No time to enjoy the present moment. Wanting to run away and hide. Feeling overwhelmed, judged, criticised and condemned.

Endometriosis
Rejecting your femininity. Devaluing yourself. Taking care of others but forget to take care of yourself. Lack of self-love, self-nurturing and self-acceptance. Dishonoring yourself. Holding onto old hurts. Not forgiving.

Epilepsy
Feeling attacked and criticised by others. Too much thinking and ignoring your feelings. Being too hard on yourself and blaming yourself for the past mistakes. Needing love and affection while trying to look tough.

Epstein–Barr
Disconnected from your own self. Carrying a lot of suppressed energy. Helping others to achieve their dreams but ignoring your own dreams. Scattered all over the place. Not being able to stick to one goal. Constantly changing your mind and can't choose what you want. Internal guilt and unexpressed aggression towards people close to you.

Eye problems:

Astigmatism

Seeing life from a distorted angle. Wanting things to be different and not accepting yourself. Holding onto rejection and resistance.

Cataracts

Having no clarity. Not trusting the flow of life. Blurred vision of the future. Resisting and rejecting.

Colour Blindness

Stressed by the vibrations of particular colours. Associating colours with childhood trauma.

Conjunctivitis

Irritated with what you see. Low self-esteem. Seeing yourself as powerless, inadequate and not good enough. Fear about the future.

Cross-eyed

Feeling guilty about what you see. Fear of punishment and pain. Blocking others from your vision field. Feeling stressed and on-guard.

Double Vision

Feeling stressed, anxious. Unclear future and unclear directions in life. Overwhelmed. Regretting about the past. Not knowing what to do. Anticipate danger.

Exotropia

Disinterested in what is happening around you. Feeling tired and spaced out. Overwhelmed. Resisting life and not trusting others.

Farsightedness

Feeling disappointed and disillusioned with life. Stuck in the past. Difficulty accepting the present.

Glaucoma

Lots of stress and fear of the future. Holding onto past hurts and disappointments. Resisting and blocking good things. Self-sabotage.

Keratitis

Too much stress. Mental and emotional exhaustion. Distrusting people. Wanting to hide. Feeling that you want to see something different from what's around you. Holding onto past hurts.

Nearsightedness
Fear of the future. Doubtful about what to do and how to do it. Not trusting your own abilities to cope.

Sty
Suppressed anger. Inability to express your feelings and saying what you want. Can't make up your mind. Low self-esteem and anxiety.

F

Fainting
Needing a way out. Stressed. Can't cope anymore. Body refused to cooperate. Out of balance.

Fat
Low-self-esteem. Using fat as a buffer to protect yourself from the energy of others. Trying to numb your feelings of unworthiness, guilt and shame. Can't make empowering decisions. Believing that you are a failure. Stuck in limiting beliefs.

Fatigue
Lost interest in life. Bored. Separated from your inner voice. Drained by too many commitments. Distracting yourself rather than connecting and listening to your body.

Female Problems
Rejecting femininity. Having negative beliefs about sexuality, sensuality and having children. Thinking that men are bad and unreliable.

Fertility
Hidden fears about becoming a parent. Holding onto unresolved childhood issues or issues with your partners. Being rigid and resisting life. Feeling jealous of people who are parents but not allowing yourself to become one. Lack of self-love and self-nurturing.

Fever
Angry with others. Tired, exhausted. Thinking of unfairness.

Fibroid Tumors and Cysts
Holding on to past hurts and disappointments. Regretting the past choices especially in regards to relationships. Not forgiving. Unexpressed creativity. Feeling you are a victim of your circumstances.

Fibromyalgia
Losing your power and becoming disempowered. Feeling stuck, unwanted, guilty and hopeless. Resistant to learn and grow. Thinking, "What's the point?" Lack of energy, loss of motivation and faith. Too much sadness and regrets about life. Disconnected from your intuition.

Flatulence
Overwhelmed with emotions. Feeling uncomfortable. Suppressing and denying your emotions rather than expressing them.

Flu
Overwhelmed with mass negativity. Believing that you have to carry the heavy burdens of others in your group. Feeling tired and stressed.

Food Allergy/Sensitivity
Very sensitive to what other people think about you. Not confident with yourself. Trying to fit other people's definition of you rather than having your own definition of yourself. Resisting life and focusing on the wrong things. Not allowing yourself to express who you are. Unresolved childhood traumas that make you deny your own power.

Frigidity
Disconnected from your own sensuality. Feeling hurt, rejected, limited, judgmental and unhappy. Carrying a lot of guilt and shame about sex. Denying bodily pleasure. Trying to control people or letting yourself be controlled by others.

Frozen Shoulder
Suppressing and numbing your feelings. Inability to express them. Going through too much stress and strain. Overwhelmed with challenges. Resisting life rather than surrendering to your life flow. Not knowing how to deal with problems. Feeling as a failure, giving up.

Fungus Infection
Irritated and annoyed with people. Family problems getting under your skin. Allowing people to control you. Inability to say 'no' to others. Holding on to beliefs that are outdated and need to be changed.

G

Gallstones
Solidified anger, resentment, and grief. Too much repressed emotions that have hardened. Carrying wounds from the past and blaming others for them. Can't forgive and let go.

Gangrene
Not enjoying life anymore. Stuck in self-distraction, self-loathing. Believing in pain and punishment. Disconnected from your inner strengths. Giving up.

Gastritis
Difficulty digesting life. Feeling sorry for yourself. Rejected, disappointed, sad. Life is too hard. Overwhelmed with life challenges. Stressed. Lack of joy, pleasure and lightness. Fear of the future.

Genital Herpes
Hating yourself. Carrying a lot of guilt and shame about sex. Feeling dirty, used, sinful, dishonoured, not worthy, violated. Difficulty forgiving.

Gingivitis
Very irritated with people and situations. Not being able to speak your truth. Unexpressed emotions pushing through the gums.

Procrastinating on taking important actions. Not enough time to nurture yourself.

Glandular Fever

Lost the connection with your own self. Feel that life is chaotic. Confused about directions in life. Allowing others to push you around. Unable to say 'no.' Lack of boundaries.

Gluten Intolerance

Problems with digesting childhood issues. Relationship difficulties. Feeling wounded and cling to your wounds. Trying to ignore your feelings and suppressing them. Disliking yourself.

Goiter

Unable to speak for yourself. Can't say what you need and what you want. Trying to please others. Avoid confrontations at all cost. Fear of rejection and criticism. Ignoring your creativity and intuition. Thinking that you should just settle with what you are given and not ask for more. Humiliated.

Gonorrhea

Carrying a lot of sexual guilt and shame. Holding onto the wounds from former relationship which didn't work. Hating yourself. Hiding your creativity. Sabotaging yourself and resisting life.

Gout

Very stressed, stubborn. Wanting to be right rather than loving. Trying to control people and situations. Very impatient and angry. Unexpressed negativity is pushing through your joints. Thinking that all things must be done your way.

Grey Hair

Believing in age, thinking 'it's downhill from here'. Stressed, feeling under pressure and strain. Lack of self-love and self-nurturing.

Growth

Nursing hurts, wounds and disappointments. Inability to express emotions and let them go. Holding onto a false sense of pride. Thinking that showing your emotions is a personal weakness. Hiding, covering up and wearing masks.

Guillain-barre Syndrome

Losing your power. Wanting to give up or give in. Thinking that you have come to a dead end. Feeling tired of life where nothing seems to work. Disappointed, hopeless and helpless. Disconnected from the flow of life.

H

Haemophilia

Family fears of pain and struggle. Vulnerability, lack of clarity and directions, instability, fragility. Rejection of the male side. Holding onto past wounds.

Haemorrhoids

Holding onto outdated family beliefs and attitudes. Can't let go and forgive. Feeling wounded and violated. Difficulty accepting new directions. Too much unexpressed anger, stubbornness and righteousness. Resisting rather than allowing things to happen. Feeling that you must prove your worth.

Hair Loss

Too much pushing and straining. Stop loving and enjoying yourself. Thinking that you are unattractive. Judging and criticising yourself and others. Pushing and resisting. Carrying guilt and resentment. Going against the flow.

Hey Fever

Bottled up feelings. Inability to express what you want. Allowing others to push you around. Feeling that you can't do what you want to do. Stuck in negative beliefs which are outdated and no good.

Headaches

You have become too stressed, too serious, judgmental, critical, tired. Too much thinking and ignoring the feelings and senses. Trying to control the uncontrollable.

Heart Attack

Blocking love and intimacy. Stuck in 'my way or no way approach.' Stubborn, obnoxious and pushy. Focusing on the material part of life, ignoring the spiritual and emotional parts. Problems with family members due to your need to be right. Feeling unloved and holding onto guilt and resentment. Selfish.

Heart Blockage

Blocking love and intimacy. Feeling unloved, separate, cut off, rejected. Focusing on the material side. Workaholic. Losing hope and faith. Thinking that being right is more important than being loved. Too hard on yourself.

Heartburn

Difficulty digesting life. Too much strain, stress and fear. Trying to push rather than allowing things to happen. Feeling wounded inside. Fear of the future.

Hepatitis

Bottled up anger. Stubborn and self-righteous. Doing things your own way only and resisting change. Easily irritated. Finding faults with people. Critical and judgemental. Holding onto past wounds. Lack of hope.

Hernia

Burdened by disappointments in relationships. Too much strain to keep your head above water. Thinking too much and not listening to your body. Believing in pain and punishment. Sabotaging yourself. Angry with people and situations. Blocking your creative expression.

Herniated Disc

Too much strain and struggle in life. Feeling that you can't hold on anymore. Burning up with emotions. Difficulty asking for help. Stuck in your own little world with no way out. Lack of self-love and self-nurturing.

Hiccups (recurring)

Not speaking your truth. Hiding what you really feel rather than expressing it. Doubtful about making the right choices in life. Indecisiveness. Stuck between the need to please people and your desire to do your own things.

Hip Problems

Carrying too much burdens on your hips. Overwhelmed with responsibilities and too many family problems. Feeling unvalued, unloved, unappreciated. Allowing others to manipulate you. Internal guilt, shame and rejection. Can't move forward.

Hives

Very irritated and annoyed. Bottled up anger, fear, and rejection. Feeling that you never get what you want.

Hodgkin's Disease

Stressed with too many commitments and responsibilities. Too much resentment, self-control and judging. Feeling obligated, trying to please others. Wanting people's approval. Rushing to achieve at all costs. Extreme fear of failure.

Huntington's Disease

Extreme disconnectedness from the self. Losing interest in life. Giving up or giving in. Feeling apathetic, depressed, lack of desire, lack of joy. Deadening inside.

Hyperactivity

Scattered, impulsive, bored, in constant need of change and stimulation. Lack of values.

Hypertension
Pushing hard to achieve. Trying to control the uncontrollable. Craving for praise and recognition. Unsatisfied with inner-self. Holding onto rage and anger. Inability to express and release your emotions.

Hyperthyroidism (overactive thyroids)
Rushing too much and not expressing your needs and emotions. Overloading yourself. Doing everything for everyone but ignoring yourself. Never enough time to enjoy life. Feeling humiliated and that you never get to do what you want. Lack of self-nurturing.

Hyperventilation
Holding on to worry, stress and negative thoughts. Feeling out of control. Overwhelmed with too many things. Taking things personally. Lack of internal focus. Scattered.

Hypoglycemia (see Low Blood Sugar)

Hypothyroidism (underactive thyroids)
Lack of desire. Loss of interest in life and feeling humiliated. Stuck in a limited world. Burdened by other people's problems. Holding back. Unable to communicate your needs and feelings. Refusing to participate in life thinking you never get to do what you want.

Hypotension (low blood pressure)
Giving up your power to others. Allowing others to control you and make decisions for you. Stuck in victimhood. Feeling disinterested, weak and tired. Wanting to hide and not expressing your talents.

I

Immune System (weak)
Too much insecurity and inner conflict. Pushing life rather than letting things unfold naturally. Allowing people to take advantage of you. Struggling not to lose control. Focusing on others and ignoring yourself.

Impotence
Feeling betrayed, angry and rejected. Judgmental attitude about sex and women. Unresolved childhood issues especially with your mother. Insecure and unsupported. Denying joy and pleasure. Low self-esteem.

Incontinence
Feeling out of control. Bottled up emotions that need to be expressed and released. Nagging guilt and shame. Holding onto past wounds. Unresolved childhood issues. Insecure, overwhelmed, struggling.

Indigestion
Difficulty digesting new experiences. Holding onto fear and anxiety. Wanting to be right rather than loved. Relationship problems that need to addressed.

Infection
Feeling invaded and attacked. Giving up. Too much stress and overwhelmed. Focusing on others and ignoring yourself.

Infertility
Thinking that there is too much struggle to be a woman. Feeling rejected and not good enough. Carrying burdens from the past and from other people. Holding onto pain and wounds. Stuck. Feeling like a victim.

Inflammation
Suppressed anger. Easily irritated and feeling impatient. Allowing others to control you. Burning up inside. Self-sabotage.

Insanity
Trying to escape and withdraw from life. Fleeing from family. Feeling unaccepted, abused, rejected, betrayed, and wronged. Can't deal with life anymore. Hopelessness and helplessness.

Insomnia

Too much tension, guilt, fear. Worrying about everything. Inability to relax. Not trusting the process of life.

Irritable Bowel Syndrome

Focusing on a negative side of life. Unbalanced, judgmental and too serious. Lost connections with joy and creativity. Trying to control people or letting people control you. Stuck in past wounds and hurts. Worrying about the future.

Itching

Too many unexpressed emotions. Not liking where you are. Unsatisfied desires, remorse. Feeling guilty and wanting to punish yourself.

J

Jaundice

Stressed, irritated, confused, angry and uptight. Feeling that you don't like where you are and want to find the way out. Misunderstood, rejected and not valued enough. Carrying a lot of ancestral fear. Holding on to past wounds which eat away at you. Resisting life rather than letting things be.

Jaw Problems

Having problems with many facets of communication. Having too much pride to discuss intimate feelings therefore, prefer to suppress and hide them. Feeling stressed and locked in an unwanted situation. Judgement, criticism, fear.

Joint Problems

Feeling overwhelmed by the responsibilities of caring for family and friends. Putting needs of others first, your own needs second. Insecure and judgemental. Stuck in outdated beliefs. Difficulty moving forward due to lack of flexibility. Righteousness.

K

Keratitis
Confused, angry, irritated. Unclear life directions. Feeling victimised, manipulated and out of control. Difficulty making decisions. Doubt.

Kidney Failure
Losing your power due to low self-esteem and blame. Holding onto wounds and overwhelmed with ancient sadness and fear. Self-resentment, hate, judgment and criticism. Unable to express your feelings clearly. Hiding your true self and wearing masks. Problems with relationships.

Kidney Stones
Too much fear, hardness, negativity and inferiority. Feeling wounded and victimised. Holding onto the past painful memories and unable to let go. Unable to trust and forgive. Stubborn, rigid and inflexible.

Kleptomania
Suppressed anger. Feeling depressed, unloved, ignored, and unaccepted. Having inner conflict with who you are. Not belonging. Needing attention.

L

Lactose Intolerance
Insecurity. Believing that life is difficult. Needing more joy, sweetness, warmth and kindness. Lack of confidence and self-love. Stuck in old thinking patterns and in outdated beliefs about love and belonging.

Laryngitis
Inability to express what you want. Denying your own needs and suppressing your feelings. Focusing on others but ignoring yourself.

Inability to say "no". Internal anger and criticism. Pushing too hard and not listening to your body. Lack of self-nurturing.

Leprosy
Rejection of self. Feeling dirty, rejected, outcast. Not belonging. Serious inner conflict.

Leukemia
Seeing life as hard, joyless and a struggle. Family problems. Keeping inside ancestral fears which won't go away. Focusing on a negative side of life. Feeling disappointed, betrayed, wronged. Very critical and judgemental. Living in the past. Can't forgive and let go.

Lips (cracked)
Insecure and not confident. Feeling bored. Not expressing what you really feel.

Lockjaw
Too much resistance. Unable to express your feelings and needs. Not liking where you are and wanting to be somewhere else. Feeling trapped, locked it. Very inflexible and critical.

Lung Cancer
Constantly pushing, resisting, and not giving yourself any credit. Trying hard but at the body's expense. Feeling wounded, betrayed and let down. Carrying bitterness, grief, anger and dissatisfaction in your chest. Lack of self-love and self-nurturing.

Lupus
Extreme insecurity, lack of confidence and low self-worth. Unresolved childhood issues. Feeling that people are taking advantage of you. Always putting others first and ignore your own needs. Never enough time to love and appreciate yourself. Too much fear, anger, resentment, criticism.

Lymphoma
Feeling insecure, unsafe, unsupported. Longing for love and acceptance by others. Pleasing people in order to get approval. Empty inside. Hopelessness and helplessness.

Lymph Problems
Feeling insecure, unsafe, unprotected. Easily influenced and used by others. Confused and lost. Unable to stand up for yourself. Low self-esteem.

M

Malaria
Feeling unsafe, insecure and out of balance with life and nature. Needing more love and nurturing from yourself.

Mastitis
Feeling helpless, unsupported and abandoned. Trapped and bound by responsibilities. Thinking that you must sacrifice and life is a struggle. Not enjoying being a woman. Putting needs of others first and ignoring your own feelings. Feeling loss of freedom.

Measles
Craving for love and attention. Processing family problems inside. Feeling attached, violated, threatened. Overwhelmed with worries and stress.

Melanoma
Feeling insecure, vulnerable and unprotected. Very dissatisfied with life, thinking, "What's the use?" Keeping lots of anger, guilt and aggression inside. Giving away your power and allowing authorities to take all charge. Not trusting yourself. Resisting to growing and expand your consciousness. Wanting to be told what to do and how to think instead of listening to your own inner voice.

Memory Loss

Having too much fear to remember. Wanting to escape. Stuck in negative thinking. Hating yourself. Not wanting to deal with things.

Meningitis

Feeling attacked, invaded, threatened. Out of balance. Experiencing inner conflict. Feeling that nothing is working out. Loss of hope and faith.

Menopausal Problems

Problems with expressing your femininity and fear of aging. Scared of no longer being wanted. Unloved and rejected. Disconnected from your creativity. Feeling sorry for yourself.

Menstrual Problems

Difficulty being a woman. Holding on to wrong beliefs about sexuality, sensuality and reproduction. Nursing childhood hurts. Fear and guilt. Feeling like a victim. Believing in pain and punishment.

Metabolic Disorders

Difficulty expressing yourself and communicating your own needs and wants. Carrying too many hurts and wounds inside. Not trusting people. Ignoring your intuitions and not listening to your own body.

Migraine

Overcommitting yourself. Trying to control people and situations. Pushing yourself. Difficulty expressing your sexuality and sensuality. Thinking that you don't get what you want in life. Resisting the flow of life. Angry and annoyed with others. Saying, "You are giving me a headache."

Miscarriage

Fear of childbirth and responsibilities. Unresolved family problems. Holding on to past hurts and being too hard on yourself. You must be soft, gentle and feminine in order to bear a healthy child.

Also, it can be because the fetus was defective and didn't want to survive.

Motion Sickness
Feeling unsafe, insecure. Fear of losing control.

Mouth Ulcers
Inability to express yourself and speaking your truth. People pleasing. Suppressed feelings of anger that erupting. Feeling stuck. Stubborn.

Multiple Sclerosis.
Stubborn and inflexible. Driven by fear. Disconnected from the self. Pushing yourself too hard in order to please others. Ignoring your own dreams and desires. Self-neglect. Thinking that you are not important but others are important. Carrying guilt and shame inside.

Mumps
Inability to express your feelings, wants and desires. Listening to others but not listening to your own self. Disconnected from your creativity. Hiding secrets inside. Ashamed of your sexuality.

Muscular Dystrophy
Hopelessness and helplessness. Wasting away your power and energy. Thinking that you are not important and not good enough. Allowing other people to control you and your life. Overwhelmed with responsibilities. Not listening to your own body.

N

Nail Biting
Anxious about your relationships with others. Irritated with a close friend or a family member. Low self-esteem. Nervous about upcoming events. Trying to please others for approval.

Narcolepsy
Trying to escape from life. Not liking where you are. Wanting to be in a different place. Bored. Disinterested. No clear directions in life. Disconnected from the self.

Nausea
Feeling trapped in a situation you don't like. Can't handle things. Fearful, traumatised, vulnerable.

Nephritis
Unresolved family issues. Ancient fears that won't go away. Carrying guilt, shame and loneliness inside. Taking too much responsibility on yourself. Disappointments with relationships and feeling of being wronged. Wanting to punish yourself.

Nervous Breakdown
Can't handle life. Have been pushed to the limit. Giving up. Feeling like a failure. Angry, betrayed, wronged, disappointed.

Nervousness
Fear of failure, judgment and rejection. Wanting to please and impress others. Lack of self-confidence. Disconnectedness from the self.

Nightmares
Suppressed negative feelings. Anger, judgment, rejection are manifesting in a dream. Need to express and release negative emotions in order to stop the nightmares.

Nodules
Solidified stress, fears, rejection and drama. Waiting for something negative to happen.

Nose (bleeding)
Reacting to other people's opinion about you. Blaming yourself and others. Thinking you don't get what you want. Angry and frustrated. Needing care and nurturing.

Nose (blocked)

Blocking your intuition. Feeling weak, irritated. Allowing others to control you. Needing your own space and time with yourself.

Nose (runny)

Pushing yourself too hard. Too much thinking and not listening to your body. Allowing your head to rule your life and ignoring your heart. Blocking your intuition. Hesitant and doubtful about your life direction. Needing more clarity to be able to move forward.

Numbness

Suppressing your feelings. Not wanting to feel. Thinking that life is too hard. Escaping rather than facing problems. Lack of self-love.

O

Obesity

Too much insecurity. Using fat as a buffer to protect yourself from others. Numbing your feelings with food. Carrying guilt and shame inside. Hating yourself. Wanting to punish yourself.

Obsessive-Compulsive Disorder

Fear. Trying to control the uncontrollable. Suspicious of everything and everybody. Don't trust. Feeling unsafe, insecure, unsupported. Blaming yourself for the past mistakes. Angry inside. Lack of self-worth and self-love.

Osteomilitis

Carrying a deep hurt inside about a major issue in life. Someone wronged you. Inability to forgive. Lost trust and confidence. Internal conflict about your belonging in this world. Sabotaging yourself.

Osteoporosis

Inability to express your needs and wants. Feeling weak, unsupported and isolated. Losing your power. Holding onto your past wounds. Carrying heavy burdens from others. Not nurturing yourself. Self-neglect. Putting yourself last.

Ovarian Cancer

Holding on to deep disappointments from the past. Unresolved family issues. Feeling betrayed by somebody who was important. Trying to please others but ignoring yourself. Rejecting your femininity and thinking that women are weak. Extreme lack of self-love.

Ovarian Cyst.

Holding on to old wounds, especially from men. Broken relationship. Hating and blaming yourself. Low self-esteem. Blocking your creative expression. Suppressing emotions such as anger and resentment. Rejecting your femininity. Feeling unloved.

Overweight

Feeling stuck. Unable to express your needs and wants. Letting people control you. Needing constant approval from others. Keeping weight on as protection from negativity. Hiding your true beauty and not letting it shine. Resisting life and can't loosen the grip.

P

Panic Attack

Feeling attacked, wronged, betrayed. Too much suppressed anger. Unresolved childhood and family issues. Thinking that life is unfair and that you must struggle to survive. Unbalanced.

Paralysis

Can't handle life. Holding on to a trauma. Unresolved family and relationship issues. Feeling unloved, betrayed, left out. Fear of the future. Can't forgive.

Paranoia

Out of control. Constantly anticipating something bad will happen. Hiding dark secrets inside. Living in fear, suspicion and blame.

Parasites

Giving away your life force to others. Feeling that people feed on you. Unable to receive love and nurturing. Pleasing people to get approval and recognition. Too much negativity, criticism and resistance. Self-neglect.

Parathyroid Problems

Disappointed with life. Inability to communicate your own needs. Fear of failure. Blaming yourself for not succeeding. Letting others control you. Feeling trapped in a limited world and wanting to break free.

Parkinson's Disease

Too much fear and resistance. Trying to control everything and everyone. Holding onto a traumatic event from the past. Can't let go and forgive. Unresolved family and relationship issues. Disconnected from the self. Lack of trust. Insecure, vulnerable, trying to please others.

Peptic Ulcer

Too much stress, worry, anxiety and uncertainty. Focusing on physical things but ignoring the spirit. Going against the grain. Emptiness inside. Lack of heart and self-love.

Piles (see hemorrhoids)

Pimples

Uncomfortable in your own skin. Feeling angry and rejected. Not liking yourself.

Pneumonia

Overload with emotions which are not expressed and buried inside. Nursing anger and frustration about people. Disappointed with life. Giving up. Thinking, "What's the point? It's all too hard..." Wanting someone else to save you. Lack of self-love and self-acceptance.

Post-Traumatic Stress Disorder

Overwhelmed with fear and anger. Holding onto the past. Stuck and unable to move on. Can't let go and forgive. Living in a prison of your own mind ignoring the spirit. Thinking too much and not listening to your body. Believing in pain and punishment. Pushing away love and kindness.

Premature Birth

Stress, impatience, discomfort. Baby doesn't want to stay in an uncomfortable or hostile environment.

Premenstrual Syndrome

Having problems with being a woman. Wanting to be more masculine because you think that femininity is a weakness. Feeling trapped, unsafe and insecure. Holding onto past hurts especially in relation to men. Unresolved family issues.

Prostate Cancer

Fear of aging and losing your masculinity. Feeling uncomfortable regarding work, finances and relationship. Focusing on the material part of life, ignoring the spiritual and emotional part of life. Trying to control others or allowing others to control you.

Psoriasis

Uncomfortable in your own skin. Feeling lost and experiencing problems with belonging. Suppressed anger that erupts. Holding onto deep hurts from the past. Self-hatred and self-punishment.

R

Rash

Insecurity and high sensitivity. Inability to express your own needs and wants. Suppressing emotions that erupt.

Repetitive Strain Injury

Not listening to your body. Pushing yourself hard. Thinking that you must keep going at all cost. Allowing other people and situations to control you. Unable to express your own feelings. Suppressing and hiding them.

Restless Leg Syndrome

Resisting todo something until you can't stand it and your legs want to move forward. Long time procrastination. Very impatient, frustrated and restless.

Rheumatism

Inflexible, stubborn, domineering. Trying to be right rather than loving. Difficulty forgiving. Seeing everything just as black and white. Stuck in victimhood. Blaming yourself and others. Hold onto anger, resentment and judgment.

Rheumatoid Arthritis

Inflexible, serious, critical and judgmental. Too much righteousness and perfectionism. Nothing is good enough. Holding onto the past hurts and wounds. Blocking creative expression and love.

Rickets

Starving for warmth, support, love and nourishment. Lack of all good things. Stuck in limitations.

Ring Worms

Somebody is getting under your skin. Irritated with people. Continuously looking for help outside yourself rather than looking within. Allowing others to control you.

Root Canal

Rejecting a part of yourself. Disconnecting from your roots and feeling that your beliefs are being destroyed. Difficulty standing up for yourself. Inability to express your feelings and ideas clearly.

Rosacea

Carrying guilt, embarrassment and shame. Feeling that you're not good enough. Pleasing others instead of exploring your own self. Putting yourself last. Hiding dark secrets which are nagging you. Doubting your actions.

S

Scabies

Becoming impatient and irritable. Infected thinking. Wanting to get out of the situation but don't know how. Internal aggression and anger. Neediness. Letting others control you.

Scarring

Reminder of the past wounds. Unresolved emotions.

Sciatica

Living in the past. Having unresolved childhood issues. Worrying about money and relationship. Procrastinating and making excuses why you can't do things. Not honest with yourself. Thinking that if you are honest, you will not be accepted by others. Fears about fitting in. Feeling overwhelmed with too many responsibilities but can't let them go. Low self-esteem and self-limitations.

Scleroderma

Self- loathing. Not wanting to participate in life. Feeling trapped and imprisoned. Powerlessness, helplessness and hopelessness. Giving up. Feeling attacked and threatened by others. Wanting to hide.

Scoliosis

Feeling insecure and unsupported. Carrying many burdens on your back. Disappointed with life and people. Holding onto past hurts. Internal conflict and anger.

Seizure

Suppressed trauma. Inability to express your feelings. Overloaded with emotions. Trying to disconnect from life and withdraw.

Senility
Returning to a childhood state to escape from life and responsibilities. Unable to deal with life issues and craving for attention. Not wanting to be present. A form of control over other people.

Shingles
Unworthiness and low self-esteem that comes from childhood. Holding onto fear and tension. Too sensitive and vulnerable.

Sinusitis
Irritation with people and wanting to keep them at a distance. Family issues and feeling angry with some of the family members. Inability to express your wants, needs and desires clearly. Carrying deep guilt, shame and sadness. Feeling worn out, needing to rest. Having an internal conflict about the direction you are going.

Skin Dry
Loss of inspiration and vitality. Feeling disconnected from your purpose. Feeling uncomfortable.

Skin Oily
Trying to please others in order to be liked. Pushing yourself hard, often against the grain. Hiding your true feelings.

Sleep Apnea
Not trusting life. Unexpressed anger and disappointments. Burning up inside. Trying to please others for approval.

Sleep Problems
Thinking too much. Holding onto unresolved problems and not listening to your body. Lots of fear and anxiety. Can't let go.

Sleep Walking
Repressed emotions re-emerge while you sleep. Hiding a dark secret inside you.

Slipped Disk
Difficulty making decisions on major issues. Struggling with security and safety. Feeling totally unsupported by life. Disappointed.

Smell (loss of)
Loss of intuition. Pushing yourself too hard. Feeling that people drain your energy.

Snoring
Stubborn. Stuck in an old way of thinking and doing. Refusing to change. Feeling that you can't express what you want and need in life. Fear of change.

Social Anxiety
Fear of being judged and criticised. Needing others approval in order to do things. Feeling abandoned and rejected. Low self-esteem.

Sore Throat
Not speaking your truth. Hiding your true feelings from others. Holding yourself back. Fear of not being accepted if you express what you really feel.

Spasm
Holding onto stressful thoughts. Fear of the future.

Spastic Colitis
Insecure, unsafe and unsupported. Can't let go stressful issues in life. Focused on problems rather than on solutions. Not trusting others. Trying to control others or letting yourself be controlled by others. Feeling attacked, let down, betrayed. Continuously being on guard and expecting the worst.

Sprain
Stressed and overworked. Too many responsibilities. Becoming impatient, irritated and intolerant. Need time to relax and centre yourself.

Stiffness
Feeling stuck and limited. Having 'My way or no way' mentality. Wanting to be right rather than loving. Inflexible and stubborn.

Stomach Ulcer
Continuously on hyper drive. Driven to produce. Competitive. Not knowing exactly what you want out of life and focusing just on the material part of life ignoring the spiritual and emotional side. Feeling rejected and let down. Not knowing how to give and receive love. Acting out of fear.

Stretch Marks
Feeling uncomfortable in your own skin. Judging and criticising yourself and your body. Paying too much attention to the external beauty rather than increasing your internal beauty.

Stuttering
Feeling insecure and unconfident. Not being able to express what you really feel. Suppressing your emotions and buying into other people's criticism and limited ideas about you and your talents.

Sunstroke
Not being careful and not taking enough care of yourself. Pushing the boundaries and having rebellious attitudes. Self-neglect.

Swelling (Edema, Fluid Retention)
Too much thinking, not enough feeling and sensing. Being stuck in negative beliefs about your life, health and success. Suppressing old grief, pain and anger which makes your body swell up. Need an emotional relief to make the swelling to go away.

Syphilis
Giving away your power to others. Feeling threatened, victimised and intimidated. Carrying sexual guilt, shame and resentment. Allowing others to use and discard you. Unable to establish healthy boundaries. Continuous self-sabotage and self-loathing.

T

Tapeworm
Feeling like a victim, helpless and hopeless. Allowing other people to control you and suck your energy. Continuously finding yourself in the middle of someone else dramas. Need to claim your power and energy back to redirecting your life.

Teeth Grinding
Stressed and overwhelmed with everyday issues. Holding on to anger and fear. Worry about the future and decision making. Can't let go and relax. In great need to unwind and redirect your life.

Teeth Decay
Inability to express yourself. Difficulty making major life decisions, Indecisiveness and procrastination. Giving up easily the things you have started. Feeling that you can't bite anymore.

Thrombosis
Sabotaging yourself. Stuck in an old way of thinking and this has become your major obstacle. Focus on the problems rather than on solutions. Having a very negative outlook. Feeling threatened and fearful. Need to change your mindset and let more joy and happiness into your life.

Thrush
Trying to control your relationship or letting others control you. Feeling angry with making wrong decisions in the past and blaming yourself. Insecure and unconfident. Wanting love and care from others but not giving it to yourself.

Tics/Twitches
Feeling fearful and apprehensive about yourself. Not liking where you are and wanting to escape from a situation. Fear of the future.

Experiencing resistance to change due to pride, impatient and superior attitude.

Tinea (ring worm)
Stuck in old beliefs that don't serve you anymore, feeling irritated, frustrated and disappointed. Thinking that you don't get what you want. Allowing others to feed off your energy. Lack of self-love and self-care.

Tinnitus
Stressed and stubborn. Doesn't want to listen anymore. Not hearing your inner voice. In great need to relax, calm down and centre yourself.

Tonsillitis
Suppressing your emotions, creativity and joy. Thinking that what you need to express is unimportant and others would not listen to you. Underestimating your talents and abilities. Needing others approval in order to do your own things. Low self-esteem.

Tourette's Syndrome
Feeling stressed, frustrated, confused and out of control. Not trusting yourself and your body. Holding onto anger, sadness and loneliness. Pushing things and resisting life rather than letting it flow naturally. Having a "Life is hard and difficult" attitude.

Tuberculosis
Too much inner turmoil and struggle. Having cruel thoughts about others. Wanting revenge. Fear of being controlled. Trying to protect yourself by hurting others first. Selfish and possessive. Overwhelmed with anger and frustration.

Tumors
Holding onto old wounds, hurts and trauma. Can't forgive and let go. Wanting revenge. Believing in pain and punishment. Experiencing

jealousy and envy toward others. Feeling unsafe, insecure and unsupported.

U

Ulcers

There is something that eats away at you. What could this be? Believing that you're not good enough, perfectionism, focusing on the material side of life and trying to produce at all cost. Disconnected from the spiritual part of life and feeling helpless and hopeless. Carrying too many responsibilities. Feeling overwhelmed and on guard. Trying to control the uncontrollable.

Underweight

Denying nourishment, loving attention and care. Wanting to punish yourself. Holding onto guilt, criticism, unhappiness and disapproval of yourself. Not letting yourself expand and grow.

Urethritis

Holding on to past wounds and hurts. Thinking that life is unfair. Feeling guilty and victimised. Acting against your beliefs. Blaming others. Feeling as a failure.

Urinary Tract Infection

Pissed off with the opposite sex or partner. Carrying a lot guilt, fear and shame. Believing that there is something wrong with you. Trying to control people or allowing others to control you. Can't express sexuality and sensuality in a healthy way.

V

Vaginitis

Carrying sexual guilt. Wrong beliefs about sexuality and sensuality. Feeling victimised and wounded by past relationship and feeling that you must punish yourself for that. Blame and anger toward yourself and others.

Varicose Veins
Inability to move forward. Feeling that you are being trapped in a situation you don't like. Believing that nothing works out for you and you must struggle. Inability to give and receive love. Focusing on the physical side of life and disregarding the emotional part. Unhappy with your job and money situation. Wanting to improve it but thinking, "it's all too hard." Overloaded with negativity and your legs can no longer support this load.

Venereal Disease
Too much sexual guilt, shame and humiliation. Believing in pain and punishment. Angry with yourself and others. Disconnected from love and internal guidance.

Vertigo
Feeling scattered, unsafe, unstable and out of control. Can't cope with life anymore. Overwhelmed with emotions. Wanting to hide or be somewhere else. Refusal to look at life from a calm and centred perspective.

Viral Infection
Feeling vulnerable, attacked and criticised. Letting others manipulate you. Not expressing your needs. Burying your emotions inside.

Voice (loss of)
Losing your power. Pushing yourself too hard beyond your capacity. Refusing to listen to your internal voice and act on it. Unclear about your feelings. Confused.

Vomiting
Your body is rejecting the stress, wrong ideas, heaviness and feeling stuck. This is a sign that what you are doing is not working and you must change.

W

Warts
Focusing on things you hate. Seeing life as ugly and hostile. Feeling you are inadequate, unattractive and not worthy of good things.

Water Retention
Holding on to negative beliefs about your life, health and success. Suppressing old grief, pain and anger. Constant self-sabotage. Stuck in family conflicts and can't move forward. Need to find a way to relive your emotions.

Whiplash
This is a sign that in some areas of life you need to change and become more flexible and expansive.

Worms (parasites)
Allowing other people to feed off you. Feeling rejected, undervalued and dirty. Not liking your own body. Believing in pain and punishment.

Chapter 7

The Secret Energy of Your Emotions. How to express, release and heal your emotions

All illnesses have an emotional component. Emotions create different energy in the body. It is proven by science that when people experience different emotions – their organs vibrate differently.

It is always possible to release emotions and become free from fears that caused the illness in the first place. This is what healing is all about.

In this chapter you will learn how emotions control your health by influencing your thinking, actions and behaviours. People who ignore, dismiss, suppress or misuse their emotions, are setting themselves up for physical illness. So I want to teach you how to deal with your emotions in a healthy and constructive way.

The techniques I'll teach you are not about eliminating emotions from your life but about understanding and transforming them. You should not try to resist or avoid feeling negative emotions. You should treat them as your most reliable indicators of how things are going on in your life. Positive emotions reassure you that things are good, negative emotions tell you that you need to change something in your life.

Two Basic Emotions: Love and Fear

All emotions we experience come from two basic emotions - love and fear. Anxiety, anger, control, sadness, depression, inadequacy, confusion, hurt, loneliness, guilt, shame - these are all fear-based emotions. Joy, happiness, caring, trust, compassion, truth, contentment, satisfaction - all these are love-based emotions.

There are different degrees of intensity of emotions, some being mild, others moderate, and others strong in intensity. For example, a mild form of anger can be felt as disgust or dismay, and at an intense level it can be felt as rage or hate.

The Most Dangerous Emotions

In regards to health, the most dangerous emotions are those that we repress and bury inside. For example, culturally it is not acceptable for us to express anger, so when we have difficult experiences we often restrain anger and hide it inside. We distract ourselves with eating, exercising, watching TV or socialising in order to not feel it and as a result the emotion becomes suppressed or buried. Suppressed emotions stay in our muscles, ligaments, stomach, heart or in other organs and body parts. They remain buried inside until we bring that emotion up, feel the emotion, and then release it. Emotions that are buried are those that normally cause physical illness.

What are other ways people use to avoid feeling their emotions?
- Pretending something hasn't happened
- Overeating or eating unhealthy foods
- Drinking of alcohol
- Using recreational drugs
- Using prescription drugs such as tranquilisers and sedatives
- Over exercising
- Any type of compulsive behaviours
- Excessive sex with or without a partner
- Always keeping busy so you can't feel
- Constant intellectualising and analysing
- Excessive reading or watching TV

- Working excessively
- Keeping conversations superficial (social talk without discussing how you actually feel)
- Wearing the mask of peace and love (being artificially peaceful and loving)

What are the Symptoms of Repressed Emotions?

Keeping emotions repressed and buried is an energetically expensive habit. You lose your energy rapidly which leads to illness and an accelerated ageing process. The following are major symptoms of buried or repressed emotions.

- Fatigue and depression without an apparent cause
- Feeling uncomfortable to speak about how you really feel
- Blowing up over minor incidents
- Desire to put someone down
- Walking around with a knot in your stomach or tightness in your throat
- Feeling angry several days after the incident
- In relationships, focusing discussions on children/money rather than talking about yourselves and the feelings
- Troubled personal relationships with family, friends, acquaintances
- A lack of ambition or motivation
- Lethargic – who cares attitude
- Difficulty accepting yourself and others
- Laughing on the outside while crying on the inside

Have you ever experienced any of these symptoms? If your answer is "Yes" than I urge you to release your suppressed emotions with the method I am going to discuss further.

How to Release your Buried Emotions

I want to show you a simple and easy to use technique to release negative emotions from your body and replace them with positive emotions. Here is the process step-by-step.

1. Find a quiet place to sit and relax
2. Put your hands on your lap and take a few deep breaths
3. Name the feeling that is bothering you. For example: "I have anger that I need to release and transform," or any other emotions such as anxiety, frustration, fear, jealousy or other.
4. Answer the question: "Where in the body is this feeling located?"
5. Put your hands on this place. For example, sadness often sits in the chest, while anger and rage affect below the waist area.
6. Breathe through this area for 2-3 minutes
7. Focus on the feeling and ask: "Do you have any messages for me?" Listen to the answers...
8. Describe the emotion: What colour is it? What shape is it? How big is it? Is it warm or cold? If the emotion was an object what object would it be?
9. Visualise it and feel it
10. Ask yourself:
    "When did I first start feeling like this? What conclusion have I drawn about myself? Does this belief system still serve me?"
11. Meditate on the feeling for a few minutes and ask yourself again:
    "If I had the opportunity to let this feeling go, could I?
    If I had the opportunity to let this feeling go, would I?
    Can I do it now?"
12. If your answers are 'yes' then use a symbolic way to let go of that feeling – feel and visualise yourself getting rid of it.
    For example, if a feeling is a dark cloud, visualise it leaving your body and you push it out with your breath. If the feeling is a hard rock, you can use your hands to take it out from your body. If a feeling is a sharp knife, pull it out of your body.

    Once you've finished, it's important to fill the vacuum with something positive.
13. Use a symbolic way to replace the old feelings with new feelings, to fill the vacuum. If you don't replace it with something else – it will come back.

Use positive emotions to fill the vacuum. Visualise a particular colour associated with this emotion and put it inside your body.

- Ask yourself: "What are the emotions I want to experience?"
- Name it. For example: "I want to experience calmness and relaxation."
- What colour do you associate with this emotion? For example: "I associate calmness and relaxation with the colour turquoise."
- To produce a particular colour, rub your hands together for 30 seconds until they are warm, spread them slightly apart and feel the 'energy ball' between your palms. Then, add on a particular colour to this 'energy ball' and feel the vibrations.
- Bring this energy into your body and fill the vacuum with the new emotion.

Note: Repeat the process if the negative feeling has moved but is not yet positive, e.g. moved from fear to anxiety but is still in the body. Sometimes you have diminished it – but it's still negative. Go through the steps again and work on removing the negative feeling and replacing it with a positive one.

How to Identify the Emotions?

When you are going through the releasing process it is important to pinpoint the emotion you experience correctly. It can be difficult for some people because they experience a whole range of negative emotions. For example, the same person can feel fear, jealousy, contempt and irritation at the same time. In this case you will need to release each emotion one by one. That means doing the process for each emotion. Here is the process to pinpoint the emotion you experience.

To identify the negative emotion, ask yourself:
"Is the emotion I experience:
- Aggressive or passive?
- Powerless or powerful?
- Negative thoughts or alarming feelings?"

Pick it from the list of negative emotions:

Negative and aggressive, powerful: Anger, annoyance, contempt, disgust, irritation

Negative and powerless: Anxiety, embarrassment, fear, helplessness, powerlessness, worry

Negative thoughts: Doubt, envy, frustration, guilt, shame

Negative and passive: Boredom, despair, disappointment, hurt, sadness

Negative and alarming: Stress, shock, tension

To identify the positive emotion you want to replace the vacuum with, ask yourself:

Is the emotion I want to experience:
-Stimulating or calm?
-Nurturing or exciting?
-Positive thought or reactive feeling?"

Pick it from the list of positive emotions:

Positive and stimulating, exciting: Amusement, delight, elation, excitement, happiness, joy, pleasure

Positive and nurturing: Affection, empathy, friendliness, love

Positive thoughts: Courage, hope, pride, satisfaction, trust

Positive and calm: Calmness, contentment, relaxation, relief, serenity

Positive and reactive: Interest, politeness, surprise

Chapter 8
Emotions and Colours

Emotions are certain wavelengths of energy felt by our body. Colours are certain wavelengths of energy seen through our eyes. Therefore the energy of colour can influence our emotions and change them. For example, it is well known that cold colours such as blue can calm a person and hot colours such as red can stimulate a depressed person.

When people are going through the process of releasing negative emotions it is necessary to replace them with positive emotions to counteract the negative energy. One way to do that is to use the power of colour because certain colours can produce certain emotions.

To utilise the power of colour more effectively I have designed "Chromotherapy Healing: The Secret Energy of Colour Cards" which can help you connect to colours easier. The cards will show you which music to listen to for each colour, which food to eat, which plant to grow, which fragrance to smell and which gemstone to carry with you for every colour.

Here I want to describe what colours people normally use to relate to positive emotions when they go through the emotional release process. I hope this helps you understand, release and transform your own emotions in a more creative way.

Please understand that these emotion-colour associations are not an exact science, you may have your own perception of how emotions link to colours, which is totally fine. These associations are subjective and I offer you only examples of how many other people who I have worked with relate to emotions and colours.

My wish is to ignite your creativity and make you feel alive when you are working with your emotions and feelings. I believe this is a true way to become an emotionally free person.

Abundance – gold
Acceptance – green, emerald
Amusement - rainbow colours (red, orange, yellow, green blue, indigo, violet)
Affection – pink, peach, coral
Calmness – turquoise
Clarity – purple, white
Courage – rose
Contentment – chocolate
Confidence – orange, red
Commitment – plum
Compassion – cherry blossom
Delight- orange, apricot
Elation- watermelon
Excitement – tangerine
Empathy – coral, strawberry pink
Faith – lilac
Flexibility – aqua
Freedom – sky blue
Forgiveness - green
Gratitude – gold or pink
Happiness –yellow
Hope – lilac
Honour – violet
Interest – lemon, yellow
Inspiration- indigo
Innocence – white
Joy- amber, auburn

Love - pink
Optimism – orange, scarlet
Passion – cherry
Peace – azure
Pride – burgundy
Politeness - silver
Relaxation – blue, aquamarine, turquoise
Recognition – magenta, plum
Relief – aqua, aquamarine
Respect – mauve
Satisfaction – green
Serenity- lavender
Strength – bronze
Surprise – magenta
Trust – jade, brown
Understanding – azure

The other way to experience emotions is by listening to certain music. We all know that music affects our feelings in different ways. For example, if you want to experience relaxation you can listen to relaxing music or if you want to become inspired you can listen to inspiring and stimulating music.

To affect your feelings and emotions you can use different body movements. To calm yourself you can start moving your body in a slow and flowing rhythm. After a few minutes of moving in this slow rhythm you will notice calmness inside your whole body and mind. To experience joy you can start playful or dance like movements and you will become more joyful. To feel excited – run, jump or shake your body vigorously and you will sense excitement.

The main thing to realise is that positive emotions can be experienced and cultivated with the help of your creativity and imagination. Don't let yourself become stagnant and stuck. Emotions are meant to keep you alive, move and flow.

Chapter 9
Understanding Negative Emotions

L ook at the picture below that shows how emotions affect the body. This picture belongs to a psychosomatic research during which people underwent medical scans when they experienced different emotions. It shows how different emotions shut down some body parts and open up other body parts.

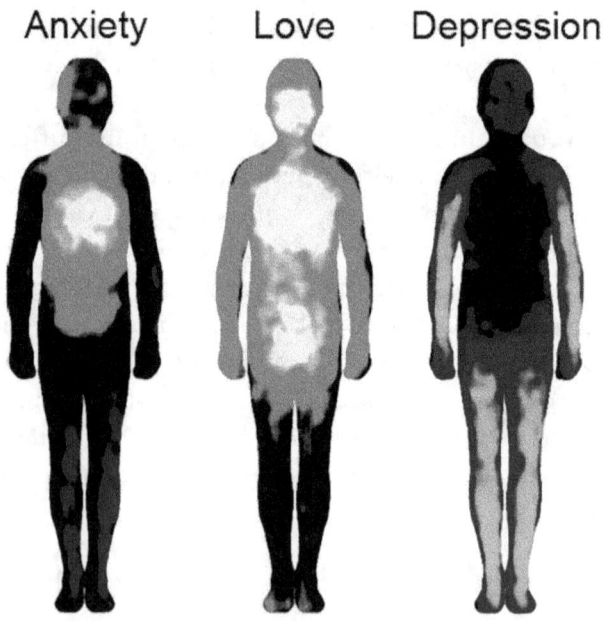

The truth about emotions is that they all are useful when we understand them.

I notice, when people describe their painful experiences, they often say, "I'm sorry for being so negative." Such reactions undoubtedly stem from our culture's overriding bias toward positive thinking. Although positive emotions are worth cultivating, problems arise when people start believing they must be upbeat all the time.

In fact, negative emotions are an important part of life, and research shows that experiencing and accepting such emotions are vital to our mental health.

Negative emotions are often natural and appropriate but it is how you express them that really determines whether they are constructive or destructive.

For example, it is natural to feel resentful when you have been left waiting by a friend who arrives extremely late without reasonable justification, or to feel sad when a loved one dies.

However, if you express your anger by yelling at someone or even ignoring them, this will probably lead to destructive outcomes.

Be aware of the negative emotions that you might experience and learn ways to understand and deal with them.

To release emotions from your body, use the 13-steps technique "How to Release your Buried Emotions" that I described in this book. This technique is suitable for all emotions listed below.

Anger:

Anger results from the thoughts or perceptions that you have been wronged. It often comes out of righteousness when people want to be right rather than loving and forgiving. When people are angry they think, "I am right, they are wrong." This gives people a false sense of power and they think they can criticise, hate, put down and resent others.

People can get angry if they don't get what they want. Anger can give a large surge of energy that can make you react in ways that you normally wouldn't. When it gets out of control it turns into rage that can have very negative consequences for you and those around you.

Long-term anger exhausts your life force and energy. This results in developing many diseases such as hypertension, heart problems, PMS, tumors, ulcers, etc. Anger can also lead to violence and psychotic episodes.

Releasing anger takes time and patience. For some people it can take a few weeks or even longer, but I deeply believe that if you do the process of releasing anger regularly, it will reprogram your nervous system and it will make you less reactive to different emotional triggers.

I recommend that you transform anger into peace and serenity and associate them with colours. Later on you should also instil the emotions of trust, satisfaction and hope into your body in order to stabilise and strengthen your nervous system.

I have researched how the energy of colors affect our emotions since my early years of being a doctor. I have created my "Chromotherapy Healing: The Secret Energy of Color Cards" as a result of my research. These cards help people to balance their five senses and become whole.

Colors - emotions associations are proven by science and you can find some of these studies in the bibliography section at the end of this book.

Attack/Criticism:

Attack/criticism costs you a lot of energy. It doesn't matter if you criticise yourself or others - criticism still drains your energy from the foundation of your body - your bones, muscles, blood vessels, immune system and internal organs. Your life becomes a chore, a burden, even miserable at times.

Long-term criticism can lead to all sort of illnesses such as arthritis, gout, frequent colds, stomach problems, nervous system disorders and many others. It also destroys your self-esteem and self-worth.

Attack/criticism arises from the lack of self-love. It can also result from the thoughts that you are no good: inadequate, incompetent, too short, too tall, too thin, too fat and the list can go on and on. When you criticise yourself it is inevitable that you will criticise others. Eventually you get stuck in a circle of continuous criticism and attack which is difficult to break.

You can transform the emotion of attack/criticism with love and understanding. Put these positive emotions into your body using the energy associated with their colours.

Control:

When people try to control others they drain their own energy, limit their opportunities, become spiritually weak and socially unlikable. They create an aura of stress and tension around themselves.

Where does this feeling come from? Control originates from the need to dominate and strive for perfection or it can come from the lack of trust in others and not believing in them. Control keeps people limited and disconnected from their hearts. It can easily turn into aggression or anger. It can suppress creativity, spontaneity, imagination and fun. Inevitably, control leads to oppression, break down, constriction and restriction.

On a physical level control can lead to brain tumors, allergies, skin conditions, eating disorders, diabetes, frigidity, gout, arthritis, irritable bowel, migraines, paranoia, female problems, Parkinson's disease, RSI, ulcers etc.

I recommend that you transform feelings of control into feelings of acceptance, satisfaction and trust.

Use the 13-steps technique "How to Release your Buried Emotions" that I describe in this book.

Depression:

Depression has become an epidemic in recent years. People often get overwhelmed with the pressures of the modern world and struggle to survive in the complexity of our society. From an energetic/spiritual view, depression is a spiritual crisis. It is a crisis of mind or a moral crisis when a person is starved for a meaningful life.

Depression can arise from disappointment, betrayal, loss of love, failure, accident, death of loved one, anger turned inwards, trauma or from feeling hopeless and helpless. Low self-esteem is a common background for depression.

Depressed people feel that they are being trapped in the darkness of their mind and unable to find a way out. However it can become an opportunity to look at your shadow side, understand yourself better and come from the angle of healing, transformation and recovery.

Long standing depression can lead to all sorts of illnesses from back pain and alcoholism to cancer.

To transform depression you need to fill yourself up with joy, love, inspiration and happiness. See the colour associated with these feelings and connect to their power.

Use the 13-steps technique "How to Release your Buried Emotions" that I describe in this book.

Failure:

Many of us have probably experienced this at one time or another. The fear of failing can be immobilising – it can cause people to do nothing, and therefore resist moving forward towards their dreams, or they may use failure as an excuse, believing that their dreams are too hard or impossible to achieve. Failure can lead to feelings of disappointment and even to helplessness and hopelessness.

However, failure can be a catalyst for change and an opportunity to discover your high potential. It's important to realise that in everything we do, there's always a chance that we'll fail. Facing that chance, and embracing it, is not only courageous – it also gives us a fuller, more rewarding life.

We can reflect on what we learned from failure and move forward with greater confidence and belief in ourselves.

To transform failure into something positive you need to fill yourself up with confidence, strength, optimism and trust. See the colours associated with these feelings and connect to them with full faith and surrender.

Fear/Anxiety/Worry:

People have fear of life because of their past experiences. From spiritual perspective fear means "false expectations appear real."

Still many people think that they are powerless victims and they have no choice but to struggle.

When people experience FEAR they are capable of betrayal, blame, lies, treachery, rejection, harm and violence. Fear incapacitates people, traps them in a darkness of negativity, stress, agitation, pretence and denial. Fear is an emotion that keeps them imprisoned, prevents their action, blocks their trust in others and stops them from achieving their goals. It continuously sabotages them, creates illusions and makes them slip into depression.

Fear impedes judgement, distorts thinking, blocks your ability to love and experience peace, joy and happiness.

Continuous fear can result in many illnesses such as ulcers, urinary tract infections, cancers, female problems, sciatica, back pain, Parkinson's, obsessive-compulsive disorder, eating disorders, diabetes and many others.

To transform fear/anxiety you need to fill yourself up with courage, love, confidence and gratitude. Checkout the colours associated with these feelings and relate to their power to heal.

Frustration/Irritation:

Frustration is common. Often people get frustrated because things didn't appear as they expected. They get impatient, irritated and stressed. They feel that the situation should be different from what it is.

At this point they failed to realise that not getting what they want is actually how the Divine guides them towards their higher good. So from a spiritual perspective being frustrated is pointless and counterproductive. You just need to be patient and grateful for the experiences you went through.

Frustration can contribute to developing problems with eyes, skin conditions, gall bladder, stomach, intestines and bowel problems.

To heal frustration/irritation you must fill yourself up with satisfaction, inspiration and clarity. Look at the colours associated with these feelings and utilise their energy to restore your body and mind.

Grief (refer to sadness/grief/loss):

Guilt

If you are experiencing feelings of guilt you are likely to be focussing on something that you have done that is embarrassing, harmful or negative. Guilt is often associated with punishment, jail and a need to serve a sentence. Certainly guilt can be a highly destructive and a damaging experience for many.

Yet, guilt isn't all bad. Guilt, in appropriate and reasonable doses, helps us all to act in ways that can be constructive, healthy and community building. Many people who experience at least a little bit of guilt are more likely to help their neighbours, care for loved ones, act honestly and with integrity, offer gracious and kind expressions to others, recycle and so forth. A little guilt helps us to do the right thing at times. It can also help us to eat better, drink less alcohol, and get regular exercise too.

Without any guilt whatsoever, we would likely have a much more challenging social environment and narcissistic world to live in.

Guilt becomes bad when we get obsessed with it and have no control about feeling guilty. It becomes a form of self-sabotage and impedes wellness. It keeps you chained rather than helping you change and discover freedom.

To transform guilt you should fill yourself up with innocence and understanding.

Hatred:

Hatred is a strong negative feeling against the object of the hate. It is an ego state that wishes to destroy the source of its unhappiness. There are many different types of hatred: There is generational hate that is passed on from generation to generation, racial hate, religious hate, cultural hate, neighbours hate. There is also personal hate based on hurt, anger and resentment. Love can turn into hate in extreme situations when people are unable to communicate their mistakes and forgive. There is family hate when family members carry strong resentment against each other due to the lack of caring and nurturing for each other.

Hatred is always bad and cause enormous suffering to those involved. It disconnects people from love, keeps them in fear, brings the worst out of them and makes them become aggressive and leads to violence.

Hatreds rot the person's body, mind and soul making them hopeless and helpless. It blocks intimacy, happiness, creativity and kindness. On a physical level it can lead to heart problems, lung diseases, hypertension, skin disorders, immune system failure and many psychological problems.

To transform hatred you should fill yourself up with love, joy, acceptance and gratitude. You must go through a forgiveness process to heal yourself from hatred. Look at the chapter "How to Forgive" in this book.

Hopelessness:

People feel hopeless when they believe they can't change the situation they are in. They feel they have no choice and it is pointless to do anything, so they would rather give up. They succumb to fear and live in despair. If you catch yourself saying, "Why bother?" you may be experiencing hopelessness. As a result of your hopelessness, you don't see your friends, you isolate yourself, you don't exercise and you don't try anything new.

You can get stuck focusing on what you can't change. On the other hand, you can look at what you can change. Let's say your relationship is hopeless, you've broken up and there is no hope to mend that partnership. So yes, that really is hopeless now, but how about other things in your life —things you can do? If the relationship or job really turned out to be hopeless, weren't you living a life before it? Start living again...like you did before.

To heal hopelessness you must fill yourself up with hope and faith. Find the colours associated with these emotions and utilise their energy to become hopeful and faithful again.

Jealousy/Envy:

Jealousy is an extremely negative emotion because it is based on wanting something other people have that you don't have or think you don't have. A big part of the problem lies within you and not with the person you are jealous of. Common causes of jealousy include:

- Lack of self-confidence. The main cause for feelings of jealousy are your doubts about your abilities or skills. If you were confident of yourself you wouldn't suffer from jealousy.
- Poor self-image. If you believe that you look bad, then you'll be experiencing feelings of jealousy whenever you meet someone who looks better than you.
- Fear. You may be afraid of being rejected or a fear of losing the love of your partner.
- Insecurity. If you feel insecure in your relationship or job, this can be a strong reason that you have become jealous.

On a physical level jealousy can contribute to digestive problems, heart attack, lung problems, tumors, back pains and many others.

To heal jealousy/envy you must fill yourself up with trust, love and faith. See the colours associated with these emotions and utilise their energy to become trusting and lovable.

You must go through a forgiveness process to heal yourself from jealousy. Look at the chapter "How to Forgive" in this book.

Judgement /Discrimination:

We all make judgements every day, whether we are buying a product or hiring an employee. But when we start to judge excessively and inappropriately, judgement can become our shadow. We start judging our family, our body, our friends, people's appearances and actions. Excessive judgements can turn into discrimination, intolerance, prejudice and conflict. Even wars can start following a harsh judgement.

When we judge others, we always fear being judged by others. Then we become controlling, stressed, irritable and angry. Judgement stops us from seeing the truth and disconnects us from love and happiness. Judgement steams from comparison that one thing is better than another. This approach makes us stop seeing the uniqueness of things and appreciating others for being the only one of their kind. It can lead to even more frustration and alienation.

On a physical level, judgement can cause laryngitis, sore throat, sinusitis, mouth problems, headaches, nervous system disorders, hearing problems and stress.

To heal judgement/discrimination you must fill yourself up with honour and compassion. See the colour associated with these feelings and use their power to heal.

Loss refer to Sadness/Grief/Loss

Low Self-Esteem/Unworthiness:

Self-esteem is how we value ourselves. Self-esteem affects our trust in others, our relationships and our work. Positive self-esteem gives us the strength and flexibility to take charge of our lives and grow from our mistakes without the fear of rejection. Low self-esteem keeps individuals from realising their full potential. A person with low self-esteem feels unworthy, incapable, and incompetent. Signs of low self-esteem include a negative view of life, perfectionist attitude, mistrusting others, a blaming behaviour, fear of taking risks, feelings of being unloved and unlovable, dependence and fear of being ridiculed.

When people have low self-esteem their body tends to break down, which can lead to acne, diabetes, weight problems, eating disorders, female problems, ulcers, cancers, memory loss and many other diseases.

To heal low self-esteem/unworthiness you must fill yourself up with confidence, trust and strength.

Overwhelm:

Most people have experienced a state of being emotionally overwhelmed at some point in their lives. Being emotionally overwhelmed can overpower a person's ability to think and act rationally. It can be caused by stress at home or work, past or current traumatic life experiences, perceived stresses and high sensitivity.

Feeling overwhelmed can sometimes be a normal reaction to very difficult circumstances. For example, if you are a single parent or unemployed and struggling to pay bills. When feeling overwhelmed, we usually react by being frantically busy, by procrastinating or by doing things clumsily or inefficiently.

Here are the questions that without fail create a sensation of being overwhelmed:
- What else have I got to do today?
- What am I forgetting?
- What else should I be doing?

These questions pull your attention away from the present. You get caught in 'not being able to take action in the present moment because you can't stop thinking about the future.'

To avoid overwhelming one's self, you need to learn to be in the now. Simply ground yourself in the present. Turn off the planning and switch on the action.

On a physical level being overwhelmed contributes to backaches, breast problems, PMS, frequent colds, frozen shoulder, glaucoma, high blood pressure, cramps, deafness, seizures, Alzheimer's, ulcers and many others.

To heal the feelings of being overwhelmed you must fill yourself up with clarity, peace and relaxation.

Rejection:

Rejection is an emotion that can stay with a person for years and cause continuous damage. It happens when one person is saying to another — "Keep away, I don't want you around me now." Such a message often hits exactly in the centre of our ego and shakes our self-worth.

After experiencing rejection people can have a fear of trusting, opening up or getting too close to people. As a result, people stop enjoying their lives and cease pursuing their dreams.

Fear of rejection contributes to the development of eating disorders, arthritis, cold sores, frigidity, female problems, nervous problems and many others.

To heal rejection you must fill yourself up with recognition and acceptance.

Resentment:

Resentment is an unexpressed hurt that becomes anger. Often these feelings target a family member or someone close to you. It comes from a thought that you have been treated unfairly or taken advantage of. Resentment greatly distorts thinking and makes it difficult to distinguish thoughts from reality. People get confused with what is right and what is wrong. Over time, resentment can become a way of life. Resentful people have to devalue others to protect their fragile egos. In relationships, it leads to some form of verbal or emotional abuse and eventually - if the couple hangs in there - to contempt and disgust.

Signs of chronic resentment in relationships:
- High emotional reactivity - a negative feeling in one partner triggers chaos or shuts down in the other
- Negative emotions are regulated by attempts to control or devalue the other.
- Automatic defensive behaviour
- Power struggles - try to "win" power
- Criticism, defensiveness, contempt
- Walking on eggshells - both parties feel this

All feelings of resentment steam from disconnectedness, ego-centric views and righteousness. Both parties normally have 'I'm right, they're wrong' attitude. They feel that resentment gives them temporary power which allows them to fight and battle each other.

Long-term resentment can lead to tumors, back problems, bones and muscles aches, fibromyalgia, osteoporosis, lupus, female problems and many more problems.

To heal resentment you must fill yourself up with forgiveness, love and trust.

You can release resentment using the 13-steps process "How to Release your Buried Emotions" that I describe in this book.

Sadness/Grief/Loss:

People often feel sad when they think they have lost something. Grief is an important part of healing. But suppressed grief and sadness can lead to depression, victimhood, hopelessness, self-pity, unhappiness and blame.

What things can create grief? It can be loss of a job, loss of a beloved pet, loss of a friendship, loss of a personal dream and loss of a romantic relationship. When people are grieving it is common to feel like you are "going crazy," have difficulty concentrating, feel depressed, feel irritable or angry, feel frustrated, experience anxiety, feel like you want to "escape," be ambivalent, feel numb and have a lack of energy and motivation.

Each person deals with grief differently and needs a different amount time to heal. However, prolonged sadness and grief can keep you stuck in the past and limit your ability to move forward.

On a physical level sadness/grief/loss can lead to pneumonia, heart problems, sinusitis, kidney problems, cysts, irritable bowel syndrome, piles, blood disorders and much more.

To heal sadness/grief/loss you must fill yourself up with happiness, joy and love.

You must go through a forgiveness process to heal yourself from grief and loss. Look at the chapter "How to Forgive" in this book.

Shame:

Shame is known to almost all people at one time or another. It may last a brief time or for some people, feelings of shame may begin in childhood and stay around until they are adults. Shame is often rooted in experiences of a sexual nature, whether consensual or not, most of the time it is related to the feelings of humiliation and fear.

Shame gives people a false sense of control over other people's feelings and behaviour. It can also protect us from other emotions that we are afraid to feel and gives us the perception of authority over our own feelings. As bad as shame feels, many people prefer it to the feelings that shame may be covering up: Loneliness, heartbreak, grief, sadness, sorrow or helplessness over others.

Shame can affect reproductive organs, lead to AIDS, genital herpes, ovarian and prostate cancer, arthritis, impotence, eating disorders, urinary infection, kidney problems, vaginitis, obsessive-compulsive disorder and other problems.

To heal shame you must transform it with the feelings of respect and honour.

Stress:

Stress is one the biggest problems nowadays. Especially for people who suffer from work related stress and personal or relationship stress. Work related stress includes being unhappy in your job, having a heavy workload or too much responsibility, working long hours, unclear expectations of your work or no say in the decision-making process, working under dangerous conditions, facing discrimination or harassment at work and much more. Personal or relationship stress includes death of a loved one, divorce, getting married, moving to a new home, chronic illness or injury, emotional problems, taking care of an elderly or sick family member and living through a traumatic event, such as a natural disaster, theft, rape or violence.

When people are stressed they normally focus on future or past events and fail to live in the present moment. Therefore, the best they can do to reduce their stress is to learn to live in the now, moment by moment.

On a physical level stress can contribute to headaches, fatigue, difficulty sleeping, difficulty concentrating, upset stomach and irritability. Long term stress can lead to more serious problems such as depression, hypertension, abnormal heartbeat (arrhythmia), atherosclerosis, heart attacks, heartburn, ulcers, irritable bowel syndrome, cramps, constipation, diarrhoea, weight gain or loss, changes in sex drive, infertility, asthma or arthritis, skin problems such as acne, eczema, and psoriasis.

To heal stress you must fill yourself up with the feelings of relaxation, peace and serenity.

Stuck:

When people are stuck, they get attached to one point of view and become inflexible. This takes place when the same thoughts or scenarios play themselves over again and again in their mind. Feeling stuck characterises stiffness, loss of creativity, constant struggle and having a 'life is hard' attitude.

To get unstuck, you must recognise where in life you are being 'stuck'. And then release these feelings and behaviours.

Feeling stuck can lead to varicose veins, sciatica, RSI, obesity, ulcers, kidney problems, diabetes, digestive problems and many others depending on where in life you feel 'stuck'.

I recommend transforming the feelings of being stuck with feelings of flexibility and movement or what you call a 'creative flow'.

Worry:

Refer to Fear/Anxiety/Worry

Please remember that all emotions can be released using the 13-steps technique "How to Release your Buried Emotions" that I describe in this book.

You will also need to go through a forgiveness process to heal your emotions. Look at the chapter "How to Forgive" in this book.

Chapter 10
How to Forgive

Forgiveness is not just important for our health, it's absolutely necessary for it. In fact, without forgiveness you can't be healed. When we forgive, we release our hurts, grow from it and change into better people. Every experience in life teaches us a lesson and only forgiveness can make us learn and accept the lesson properly.

Forgiveness is difficult. Many people try to say that they have forgiven but, in fact, they have not.

You will know that forgiveness has begun when you recall those who hurt you and feel that nothing should be any different, that everything has happened for the right reason and you have learned a great lesson from the incident. You feel grateful to the person for the experience and have the power to wish them well.

If you still feel uncomfortable when you think of the person or of the incident – you haven't forgiven yet. You still need more time and do more work to forgive and let go.

But don't worry, it will come to you. Most likely your ego is still clinging to old hurts, as it always has. To forgive, you must surrender to a power higher than yourself, the power I call Intuitive Healing Power or Divine. After your surrendering to this power, forgiveness comes naturally.

The Steps to Forgiveness!

Many people want to forgive but they don't know how. Here are the steps of the process on how to forgive, it's very powerful. For better result you should forgive one person at a time.

Follow these steps:

1. Call for Divine help, say:
   Intuitive Healing Power, I call on you to come to me and help me forgive.
   I call on my Soul and Divine self.
   I call on my guides, teachers and angels who love me unconditionally.
   Thank you for your unconditional love, support and protection.
   Thank you, Thank you, Thank you…

2. Connect yourself to the Divine pillar of light: This starts from the Divine (cosmos, universe) and enters your body through the top of your head. Meditate on this connection for 2-3 minutes.

3. Think of a person you need to forgive: Visualise him/her.

4. Say, "I call on the spirit of … (name of the person)." Call 3 times.

5. Say, "Thank you for being here and clearing our energy today."

6. Say, "(Name), I now forgive you for everything that you have ever done to me that has hurt me in this or any other lifetime. I forgive you, I forgive you, I forgive you…" Breathe in and release.
   Repeat this step 3 times.

7. Now attend to the other side of situation: What you may have done to them.
   "(Name), I now ask that you forgive me for everything that I have ever done that has hurt you consciously or unconsciously in this or any other lifetime. Please forgive me, please forgive me and please forgive me." Breathe in and release.
   Repeat this step 3 times.

8. Imagine lines of energy joining you to the other person. Raise your hand and bring it down like cutting the ties and say, "I set myself free and reclaim my spirit now. I proclaim that all karma between us ended by my sincere act of forgiveness. May you be free and may all good things happen to you. Thank you, thank you, thank you..." Breathe in and release.
   Repeat this step 3 times.

9. Give thanks to Divine:
   Say, "Intuitive Healing Power thank you, thank you, thank you..." Breathe in and release.
   Repeat this step 3 times.
   Forgiveness will empower you and heal you. Forgiveness is love, it will make you strong, powerful and enlightened.

Note: Often, the person you need to forgive the most is you. Forgiving yourself is no different to forgiving the other person. You need to go through the same process and follow the same steps. Visualise yourself as you would visualise any other person. When you need to cut the energy line, cut the energy line between the version of you who caused the problems and the new version of you who is asking for forgiveness.

AFTERWORD

I am very grateful for the opportunity to do what I am doing. Every day I start with expressing the words of gratitude and love to those who surround me and who give me strength, courage, inspiration and love.

It is difficult for me to express in words the gifts and benefits I have received from the realisation that I can not only heal myself but help others to release their fears, transform their life, heal their energy and become stronger. I observe incredible miracles every time I work with people and they realise that they don't need to suffer or struggle anymore, and that they have their own power to heal and transform their life.

Through my work I discovered that all people, doesn't matter where they are in the world, desire similar things – good health, happiness, joy, connection, peace of mind, love, abundance and freedom. I only wish that more and more people can realise that and see how we all are connected. We all have incredible wisdom and intelligence inside ourselves called Intuitive Healing Power. All people need is the tools and knowledge of how to listen to their intuition, especially their health intuition. Then our world and our planet can be transformed, healed and nourished using the good energy of the human soul. I would love to hear your feedback and your stories of how, "The Secret Energy of Your Body" has changed your life. Please contact me through my website http://dririnawebster.com/ May the Intuitive Healing Power run through you and lead you to discover the secret energy of your mind, body and spirit.

With Love,
Dr Irina Webster

ABOUT AUTHOR

Dr Irina Webster is a medical doctor with a degree in Women and Children's Health. She has practiced conventional medicine for 15 years in two countries: Russia and Australia. Here is her work history...

Dr Irina graduated from Northern State Medical University (Russia) in 1993 obtaining the qualification of doctor-paediatrician. In her early years of being a doctor she had a great interest in immunology and even did her post-graduation studies in this field acquiring a qualification of Immunologist –Allergist from the Medical University of Saint-Petersburg (Russia). This 7 year practice in immunology gave her lots of insight in human immune system and how our body gets protected from certain diseases.

During her postgraduate studies she had her first connection to a new science called Psychoneuroimmunology (Psycho means psyche, neuro is for nervous system and immunology is for immune system). From there Dr Irina learned that what happens in our minds at the level of our perception can have real effects on our immune system and the rest of our body and organs.

Psychoneuroimmunology research shows that negative thoughts, beliefs, attitudes and emotions weaken the nervous and immune systems and lead to disease.

Dr Irina collected scientific data about emotional patterns and illness since 1994 and brought her research from Russia to Australia. This book is based on her original research.

This concept is not new, and the ancient wisdom has always encouraged us to focus on maintaining a 'healthy' mind in order to maintain a healthy body.

When she moved to Australia in 2001 she became interested in eating disorders and addictions. This area has always kept her interested due to her personal problems with eating disorders, so she finally decided to undertake some work and research in this field. As a result Dr Irina has written 2 books about eating disorders, created specialised meditation CDs for eating disorders and an audio program for anorexia-bulimia sufferers.

Working with people who have eating disorders helped her understand the mind and the brain and how the suppressed emotions create addictions and other health problems.

Her other interests include fertility and pregnancy (her best-selling book "Healthy Pregnancy from A to Z") because fertility is a common problem amongst eating disorders suffers and women with addictions.

While doing her work in these areas (and from her personal experiences with health problems) Dr Irina realised that real healing and recovery from any illness or condition came from inside of the person – from accessing and using your own intuitive healing power.

Now Dr Irina devotes all her work to helping people realise their own intuitive power and intuitive healing abilities. She is a creator of Intuitive Healing Power – an educational program for health professionals and caregivers in regards to intuitive healing and medical intuition.

BIBLIOGRAPHY OF DR IRINA'S RESEARCH

These are scientific documents that show How Emotional Patterns affect Organs:

- Brown, G.W., et al., *"Social Class and Psychiatric Disturbance Among Women in an Urban Population,"* Sociology 9, no. 2 (May 1975): 225–254.

- Naz Kaya, PH.D Assistant Professor; Helen H. Epps, PH.D.; Professor: Dawson Hal *"Relationship Between Colour and Emotion: a Study of College Students"* 1982

- Li-Chen Ou National - Taiwan University of Science, Ming Ronnier Luo - Zhejiang University, Andrée Woodcock - Coventry University, Angela Bridget Wright *"A study of colour emotion and colour preference. Part I: Colour emotions for single colours"* June 2004

- Goodkin, K., et al., *"Life Stresses and Coping Style are Associated with Immune Measures in HIV Infection— A Preliminary Report,"* International Journal of Psychiatry in Medicine 22, no. 2 (1992): 155–172.

- Jackson, J.K., *"The Problem of Alcoholic Tuberculous Patients,"* in P.J. Sparer, *Personality Stress and Tuberculosis"* (New York: International Universities Press, 1956).

- Asia Pacific International Conference on Environment-Behaviour Studies, Salamis Bay, Conti Resort Hotel, Famagusta, North Cyprus, 7-9 December 2011, *"Environmental Colour Impact upon Human Behaviour: A Review"* Nurlelawati Ab. Jalila*, Rodzyah Mohd Yunusb & Normahdiah S. Saidc

- Schmale, A.H., *"Giving up as a Final Common Pathway to Changes in Health,"* Advances in Psychosomatic Medicine 8 (1972)

- Sarason, I.G., et al., *"Life Events, Social Support, and Illness,"* Psychosomatic Medicine 47, no. 2 (March– April 1985)

- Thomas, C.B., and K.R. Duszynski, *"Closeness to Parents and Family Constellation in a Prospective Study of Five Disease States,"* The Johns Hopkins Medical Journal 134 (1974)

- Mason, J.M., *"Psychological Stress and Endocrine Function,"* in E.J. Sachar, ed., Topics in Psychoendocrinology (New York: Grune & Stratton, 1975)

- Reiter, R.C., *"Occult Somatic Pathology in Women with Chronic Pelvic Pain,"* Clinical Obstetrics and Gynecology 33, no. 1 (March 1990)

- Slade, P., *"Sexual Attitudes and Social Role Orientations in Infertile Women,"* Journal of Psychosomatic Research 25, no. 3 (1981)

- Weil, R.J., and C. Tupper, *"Personality, Life Situation, and Communication: A Study of Habitual Abortion,"* Psychosomatic Medicine 22, no. 6 (November 1960)

- Alvarez, W.C., *"Nervousness, Indigestion, and Pain"* (New York: Hoeber, 1943)

- Dunbar, F., *"Emotions and Bodily Changes"* 3d ed. (New York: Columbia University Press, 1947).

- Alexander, F., ***"Psychosomatic Medicine"*** (London: George Allen & Unwin, Ltd., 1952)

- Bacon, C.L., et al., ***"A Psychosomatic Survey of Cancer of the Breast,"*** Psychosomatic Medicine 14, no. 6 (November 1952)

- Kalis, B.L., et al., ***"Personality and Life History Factors in Persons Who Are Potentially Hypertensive,"*** The Journal of Nervous and Mental Disease 132 (June 1961)

- Krantz, D.S., and D.C. Glass, ***"Personality, Behavior Patterns, and Physical Illness,"*** in W.D. Gentry, ed., Handbook of Behavioral Medicine (New York: Guilford, 1984).

- Booth, G., ***"Psychodynamics in Parkinsonism,"*** Psychosomatic Medicine 10, no. 1 (January 1948)

- Cloninger, C.R., ***"Brain Networks Underlying Personality Development,"*** in B.J. Carroll and J.E. Barrett, eds., Psychopathology and the Brain (New York: Raven Press, 1991)

- Groen, J.J., ***"Psychosomatic Aspects of Ménière's Disease,"*** Acta Oto-laryngologica 95, no. 5–6 (May–June 1983)

- Mitscherlich, M., ***"The Psychic State of Patients Suffering from Parkinsonism,"*** Advances in Psychosomatic Medicine 1 (1960)

- Adams, D.K., et al., ***"Early Clinical Manifestations of Disseminated Sclerosis,"*** British Medical Journal 2, no. 4676 (August 19, 1950)

ALSO AVAILABLE FROM DR IRINA WEBSTER

"How to Heal Using Intuitive Healing. A journey to a whole you."
By Dr Irina Webster

"Have you found yourself resonating with the new scientific evidence released by neuroscience recently, which has proven that under the right conditions, the body has the power to heal itself from even the most 'incurable' illnesses?

The key words here are – 'under the right conditions' ... What are these conditions and how do we create them?

- Intuitive Healing helps creating these conditions by making you aware of your innate ability to understand your own health and wellbeing.
- Have you heard a saying "Nobody knows your body better than you..." If you could only listen to your Health Intuition – you can heal any problems, prevent illnesses and be well.

This book will help you become attuned to your own Intuitive Healing voice and will help you create the right conditions to heal."
Available from http://dririnawebster.com

'Chromotherapy Healing' cards.
By Dr Irina Webster
47 cards and a guidebook

'Chromotherapy Healing' cards are your unique tool to unlocking the extraordinary healing power of colour. Colour healing can be used very effectively to treat many problems: Physical, emotional, and spiritual.

Dr Irina Webster has researched how to balance 5 senses (visual, hearing, smell, taste, touch) in order to heal your body and soul. The cards will show you:

- What colour to wear each day to help yourself heal
- What gemstone to carry with you to evoke the energy of each colour
- What music to listen to in order to sense each colour
- What smell can help you connect to a particular colour
- What food to eat to feel the energy of each colour
- What plants to grow in your garden to enhance the power of each colour.

Available from www.dririnawebster.com

Intuitive Healing CDs and guided Meditations.

1. **'Overcome Stress Naturally with Intuitive Healing.'**
   Guided Meditation (1-hour)
   This CD will help you to overcome stress naturally using your own intuitive healing power. Step by step you will be guided to heal yourself.

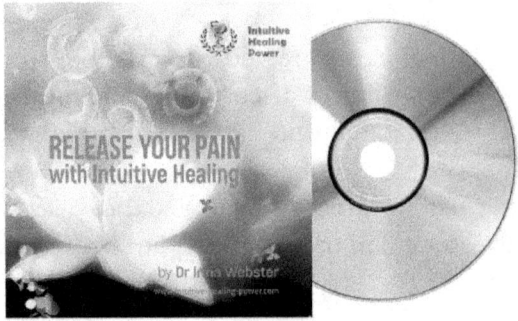

2. **'Release Your Pain with Intuitive Healing.'**
   Guided Meditation (1- hour)
   This CD will assist you to activate your own intuitive healing ability and help to relieve pain naturally. You will be guided to clean out the blockages and the densities from the place that is in pain. You will also be guided to heal negative emotions and create more joy, happiness, and pleasure in your life.

3. 'Body Scan Meditation with Intuitive Healing.'
Guided Meditation (1-hour)
The purpose of body scan meditation is to study the entire body, part by part. It is like going through your whole body with an x-ray machine checking organ by organ, muscle by muscle and bone by bone.

4. 'Progressive Muscle Relaxation with Intuitive Healing.'
Guided Meditation (1-hour)
Progressive relaxation helps you control the state of tension in your muscles. Step by step you'll be guided to relax and experience a joyful and loving state.

Available from www.dririnawebster.com

'Healthy Pregnancy from A to Z: An Expectant Parent's Guide to Wellness.' Book

By Dr Irina Webster
Intuitive Pregnancy Book.

Pregnancy is a highly intuitive time in a woman's life. Your intuition or 'six sense' naturally increases and you can use this to stay healthy and vibrant. More importantly, you can connect to your baby and keep this sacred bond from the time of conception and even earlier.

> Pregnancy and Intuition.
> Mother and Baby Intuitive Bond.
> Father and Baby Intuitive Bond.

Questions arise such as what is healthy to eat? Should I exercise and how? What lifestyle should I have? What to believe in while pregnant? What about relaxation and maintaining good relationships? Are pre-pregnancy preparations important?

This book is a deep exploration of the most important question, 'How to Be Healthy during Pregnancy?' And it shows you a way to health and wellbeing while expecting a child.

By reading this book, you will discover:

- Five Healthy Pregnancy Principles.
- The healthiest things to do each month during pregnancy.
- Your baby's development, what they can do and what they can sense each week throughout the duration of the pregnancy.
- Twenty-one Best pregnancy foods.

- How to maintain your sex life during pregnancy.
- Seven healing meditation techniques for pregnancy.
- Special exercise complexes during pregnancy.
- Beneficial yoga poses for different stages of pregnancy.
- Thirteen ways to bond with your unborn child.
- The safe herbal remedies to heal pregnancy complaints.
- Natural ways to keep your skin, hair, and teeth beautiful during pregnancy.
- How to love your pregnant body.
- Several techniques on self-massage to heal and rejuvenate you during pregnancy.
- How a father-to-be can be a loving partner and a caring dad.
- How to quit your bad habits during pregnancy.
- How music can benefit your pregnancy and what kind of music you should avoid when expecting.
- Steps to ensure a healthy birth and fast, natural recovery.

On-line Courses and Professional Trainings:

5 WEEKS TO FORGIVENESS: HOW TO FORGIVE COURSE

In this course you will learn:
- Essential steps in How to Forgive.
- How to Forgive yourself.
- Forgiveness using Past life experiences.
- Energy Anatomy of Forgiveness.
- Fill your heart with Loving-kindness.

Available from www.dririnawebster.com

HOW TO MAKE AN INTUITIVE DIAGNOSIS

- How to make an intuitive diagnosis on yourself and on other people.
- How to make an intuitive diagnosis before you see a client and then, when you are with a client.
- How to read the body signs and interpret them.
- How to read people's names.
- How to scan the body energetically.
- How to ask your intuition for help and guidance.
- How to interpret your intuitive impression.

Available from www.dririnawebster.com

HOW TO SCAN YOUR OWN BODY WITH ENERGY MEDICINE

In this course you will learn how to:

- Scan Your Own Body layer by layer like a x-ray vison.
- Identify the energetic blockages in the body and release them.
- Activate your, 'inner eye' – the natural ability to see your body from the inside.
- Sense the, 'subtle body energy' inside the organs.
- Scan the body of other people (after learning how to scan your own body).

Available from www.dririnawebster.com

HOW TO TALK TO YOUR BODY AND ORGANS

In this course you will:

- Learn to connect to your own organs.
- Learn to understand your body's (organs) messages.
- Learn to sense the subtle body energy.
- Learn to communicate with your own body.
- Learn what different body shapes tell us.

Available from www.dririnawebster.com

HOW TO REMOVE EMOTIONS FROM THE BODY

In this course you will learn:

- How to identify where in the body the emotions are trapped.
- How to remove the trapped emotions from the body/organs.
- How to balance the organ(s) after releasing the trapped emotions.

Available from www.dririnawebster.com

BECOMING AN INTUITIVE HEALER AND A MEDICAL INTUITIVE

In this course you will learn how to:

- Connect to organs and sense energy in the organs.
- Body scan on yourself and others.
- How to make an intuitive diagnosis.
- How to read the body.
- How your hands can heal you.
- Human Energetic Anatomy and how to use it for diagnosis and healing.
- Reading intuitive information from people's names.
- Working with Healing dreams, hypnagogic states, and lucid dreaming.
- How to ask your intuition for help and guidance.
- How to interpret your intuitive impressions.

Available from www.dririnawebster.com

"CURE YOUR EATING DISORDER:
5 Step Program to Change Your Brain.
Neuroplasticity Approach." Book
By Dr Irina Webster

What are the 5 Neuroplasticity Steps that will stop any Eating Disorder (even the most long-standing ones)?

1. Believe that you can stop your bulimia disorders
   Do exercises to begin changing the way your mind works.
2. Re- Identify
   Recognise the false nature of your bulimia disorder thoughts.
3. Re-Symbolise
   Escape from loop thinking that feeds the bulimia disorder.
4. Re-Direct
   Defeat recurrent thoughts that give power to the bulimia disorder.
5. Re-Evaluate
   De-value and ignore harmful urges until they start to fade away.

Once you learn and practice these five steps, your eating disorder will start to fade away.

The book will make you able to:

· Make permanent positive changes to the structure and function of your brain associated with stopping eating disorder behaviours.

- Stop the little voices in the head that tell you to starve or binge and purge.
- Change your feelings and sensations to the best so that you don't have to use an eating disorder to make up for them.
- Stop the, 'broken eye syndrome' – when you see a fat person in a mirror when you are actually very slim.
- Have control over your anorexic or bulimic thoughts and be able to tune them out of your brain.
- Restore your feelings of hunger and of fullness sensations.
- Restore your self-esteem, feelings of control and decision-making abilities.

Available from http://www.eating-disorders-books.com/

www.ingramcontent.com/pod-product-compliance
Lightning Source LLC
Chambersburg PA
CBHW071605080526
44588CB00010B/1025